A Journey to Love

A Holy Quest in southern France

Mieke Vulink

www.miekevulink.nl
Mystical initiation pathways, spirituality and sacred journeys

A Journey to Love
Author: Mieke Vulink
Translation: Marianne van Mierlo and David Lorimer
Literary Agent and Editor: Wendy Yorke, WRITE.EDIT.PUBLISH
www.wendyyorke.com

© 2022 Mieke Vulink
Published in Dutch, Zutphen
2023 Published in English

Paperback ISBN: 979-8-9882981-1-3
Hardcover ISBN: 979-8-9882981-3-7

EBook Formatting: weformatbook
Cover Designer: Natasa Ivancevic
English Version Publishing Guide: Parul Agrawal, Serapis Bey Publishing

September 2015, 1st edition
October 2016, 2nd edition
June 2019, 3rd edition
December 2019, 4th edition

May this book encourage, inspire and give you trust
on all pathways to your personal, universal
and divine consciousness.

Table of Contents

PART THREE:
THE NETHERLANDS

♥

The masculine & feminine Holy Heart, Villa Bethania, Rennes-le-Château

Preface

Our life on planet Earth can be seen as a long walk, without clearly knowing where we are going. During this walk we meet people, animals and situations that help us to experience, to learn but also, to remember. When we proceed in our spiritual awakening and experience more and more in our personal consciousness, we can see that this walk isn't just going anywhere, it is actually clearly directed. We discover that certain experiences all have a goal and are not based on coincidence. You will even remember places that you have been to before, on earlier walks, in earlier lives.

The fact that we are walking on this planet Earth is not by chance either because the Earth (Gaia) took it upon herself to allow us to experience all facets of love here.

If we added up all our walks here on Earth in one journey, you could call this travel diary, *A Journey to Love*.

For me, it feels that when we have finished with our walks on this Earth, we evolve further to the next place in the Universe. This is when we have written the last page of our own, *Journey of Love*.

Mieke takes us, in all openness, on a small part of her walk; a mother and daughter on a journey to Montpellier in France and from there to Rennes-le-Château. A journey in which past and present are mingled and come together.

The memories there don't come naturally; many years of Mieke's self-work have preceded this. It also requires huge courage and perseverance because these memories bring to the surface much pain, sadness and doubt. Sometimes, the magnitude of all this is hard to grasp or to bear.

Mieke shows us, by sharing her memories that the connections with the Light World are always there. They have always been there, even though we don't always experience it that way. She also reveals a small glimpse into the *Book of Love*, as Yeshua and Mary Magdalene wrote it; a book that in my view can be opened up and read by more and more people.

Her travel book can also dissolve the loneliness of those people who feel deeply connected with the Essenes, Cathars, Templars, Yeshua and Mary Magdalene; giving them the faith that their deep feelings are real and will be remembered and expressed by an increasing number of people.

Have a pleasant walk!

Vincent Rikkerink

Therapist, healer and husband

♥

Jan Graham
about A Journey to Love

There is no doubt about it; *A Journey to Love* asked to be written! This book reveals a classic example of how faithfulness and obedience to an inner calling can lead you on a journey that leaves you in a state of awe and wonder.

The reader can be no less affected as, page after page, Mieke Vulink affirms through her direct experience that when a vocation is followed, grace is present at every turn to inject oil into the wheels of endeavour. Mieke and her daughter Eva's journey, through the Languedoc area of France on the path of the Holy Grail, provides a story that neatly entwines many different threads.

It is firstly, an informative travel log through one of the most beautiful and sacred corners of Europe. Even someone who is uninitiated in the histories and mysteries of the region cannot fail to be drawn to. At the same time, it provides a perfect guide to anyone interested in exploring the sacred sites with their own associations with the Essenes, Cathars, Templar Knights and medieval history.

Like a complex jigsaw puzzle, the story unfolds as chance encounter followed by inner visions and intuitive hunches followed by another chance encounter draws together a collection of characters who each have a crucial role in leading to the *dénouement* and ultimate encounter at the end of the book.

Mieke has that special ability to allow her inner guidance to bring her always to the right place, at the right time, to meet the right people. Sometimes that means to be sitting at the right restaurant table, to have her ears flapping in the right direction to overhear the right conversations.

But most fascinating is where Mieke cleverly weaves together the directional and the dimensional elements as she and Eva allow themselves to be guided to one of the most wonderful stories in Christian history. The Holy Grail, the quest for it and the real and mystical meaning of it. Inseparable from that of course, are Yeshua and Mary Magdalene who are Mieke's inspiration and whose love is her companion on her journey.

One of the cleverest parts of Mieke's writing is that, in spite of the obvious input of unseen forces with which she co-creates her pilgrimage, she never becomes overly poetic or ungrounded. Even when describing her own sublime and profound mystical experiences, she reveals enough to give the reader a taste of what she went through while never losing her perspective of the detached observer.

Mieke Vulink is a modern-day mystic. This becomes clear as she shares with her reader insights into her occasional doubts and fears as she bows down before the enormous implications of what she experiences. In her writing, legend becomes truth.

Scottish born Ian Graham is a spiritual coach and healer. He has worked for nearly forty years as the channel for White Bull. He is the author of two books about the wisdom of White Bull. He regularly facilitates retreats on Patmos Island, Greece and journeys to the Himalayas.

PART ONE:

The Netherlands

Show me the Way, Kirk Richards

Coming Home, Finally

It started in November 2013, when Mieke of the Essenes emerged fully. After I had settled down in my small, new rented house, I vowed that I would allow myself to come home to Earth. The Essene part of me could remember the wise, dignified woman I once used to be. I had been looking for her for some time in this life.

When Hans Stolp (a famous and loved Dutch writer and speaker of Esoterism) talked about their existence, in one of his lectures that I had attended in 2005, the Essenes became a magical code for me. By letting their existence resonate within me, tears always started to flow and I was taken into another world, which I somehow knew used to be mine.

After having read a few books about them, I attended another of Hans' lectures. During a coffee break, I approached him at the table where his books were on show and I asked him whether he could recommend another worthwhile book about the Essenes; those dedicated people in their linen robes, from the Carmel and Qumran; they all continued to intrigue me. Hans looked me in the eye and said; "I think you should write a book about them". Slightly taken aback, I smiled and muttered something inaudible like; "I'm not ready for that yet".

Now, settled in this lovely quiet place at the IJsseldijk, in the Netherlands, I felt that, I had become ready for this challenge. However, I wasn't ready yet to write a book about the Essenes, but on the inside, I was ready to make the big journey within. Or at least, to go back to the Essene world that was hidden within my deepest layers, behind several personal shadows. After twenty-five years of transformational work, I had become used to inner work and was no longer afraid of whatever wanted to show itself from within my personal unconscious layers.

And what a thorough journey inwards it was! In total solitude and far away from Earthly temptations – helped enormously by temporary legal assistance - I started to rediscover my true self; Mieke of the Essenes. Thank God there were books that touched something within me from different angles and which awakened something deeper within me as I started to remember.

Fortunately, Herbert van Erkelens (who also wrote a book about the Essenes) introduced me to two books that he had written together with a certain Judith Moore. In her book, *De Spiegel van Magdala/The Mirror of Magdala,* she writes as a messenger from Mary Magdalene, about lost archives with forbidden knowledge that hold a key to create a new world; a world of compassion.

Mary Magdalene was initiated by Jesus (whom I will call Yeshua from now on, his original Aramaic name) into a forbidden Kabbalah and she left Israel for the south of France after the crucifixion.

It was safe there, with many Essenes and Celtic Druids living in the area who had a good connection with the Holy Family. In the Languedoc, she received visions and gospels of the Living Alliance. Reading this, I became conscious of how every human being has to walk their own path of fear, sadness and pain; through the darkness of the Earth, to come home again to our divinity and our brightest light. Exactly as Mary Magdalene and Yeshua had done.

Mary Magdalene in France

16

I couldn't let it go. Together with a then befriended colleague Vincent Rikkerink I researched anything that had to do with this holy path taken by Mary Magdalene and Yeshua; and how to translate this to the path that we ourselves are now walking, 2000 years later. Their path definitely wasn't the path described in the Bible. Their path was a unique path involving many years of surrender and self-research. It involved initiations in hidden mystery schools that have carefully kept and safeguarded this pure esoteric knowledge through all this time and passed it on, with roots in Lemuria, Atlantis, Egypt, Israel, Asia Minor and India. It required a life-long dedication and a secluded life, in communities that served the all-compassing divine plan with their lives and kept the light on Earth alive.

For me the process of inner transformation went on day and night. The more layers I went through, the stronger the original knowledge returned to me. But also, the more persistent the personal blockage and layers of pain were, which had ingrained themselves between me and this knowledge.

In the summer of 2013, I went to a theme day about Mary Magdalene given by Nanco Immanuel – a Dutch friend and an activator of higher consciousness. He was talking about a spiritual group tour he was about to lead to the Rosslyn Chapel near Edinburgh, in Scotland, I knew immediately that I had to go too. Also, this tour would start on my birthday in August; this was meant to be!

By the end of August, I was standing at the reception in the Rosslyn Chapel. I said that I wanted to go into the chapel every day for the next few days, to be able to feel and meditate by myself when the group had left. I was given a free entry pass for the coming days! For me this was a sign from the Light World.

It actually did make sense to go back there four times in a row, to align with the esoteric knowledge and the divine love that are both abundantly present there.

During one of those last days there was a loud American couple having breakfast in my otherwise peaceful and quiet B&B. I was in a meditative state and preferred silence, but whatever I tried, I

The Rosslyn Chapel, Edinburgh, Scotland

wasn't able to close myself off from their squabbling.

I understood that they had missed a bus that should have taken them to visit several highlights in Edinburgh. Now, they had to plan the day by themselves and they couldn't make up their mind where to go. When I heard the word chapel I got up, as if urged by something within me and I walked across to their table. When I got there, I didn't exactly know what to do, so I started talking about the Rosslyn chapel, about how special and impressive it was.

This incident took a beautiful turn, when the woman fell silent, observed me like she saw right through me, and spoke.

"Do you know the books of Kathleen McGowan? If I were you, I'd start reading them."

I had never heard of her before. But, once back in the Netherlands, my walk to that breakfast table turned out to be a big hit.

Together with the three thick mystery books written by Kathleen McGowan about Mary Magdalene, Yeshua and the Medici, I embraced the autumn.

I had voluntarily entered the legal aid system. I'd already known for a few years that I wouldn't be able to hold up my business practice, which I'd held together financially mainly by giving piano lessons.

Love Conquers Death, in the Rosslyn Chapel Garden, Edinburgh, Scotland

Now, my heart had started beating more and more insistently for the path of self-realisation. The Earthly work had to make way for my inner journey. I had lots of time to pull back from what the outer world wanted of me. Even though a part of me didn't agree and had fears and doubts, I extended my antennae towards a world beyond duality.

In the Sacred Valley, Rennes-le-Chateau, France

Standing alone doesn't mean
I am alone
It means I am strong enough to
handle things all by myself

The unseen world became virtually my only conversation partner for months. I went through piles of handkerchiefs and couldn't stop either reading or crying. I came home within myself and felt so carried by the all-compassing love of Mary Magdalene and Yeshua. Sometimes, it was like the Holy Family were riding past my house on the dike, touching me and encouraging me to go further on this track.

One morning, I received a phone-call from my friend Marianne. She had come to live in the same park a few months after me, in February 2014. Oddly enough, she turned out to be on practically the same inward journey as I was. This led to a special friendship. What a blessing it was to find a fellow traveller! She told me that her sister had invited her to attend a reading with an American woman who could look through your past lives, to align with your DNA and read your complete divine plan. She asked me whether I wanted to come with her, to be her translator.
"Of course," I said, knowing that a session like this would always touch my own inner path. "Who is this reading with?"
"Oh, you probably don't know her. Her name is Judith Moore."
I sat up in my chair and felt the goosebumps over my whole body and I knew, *Now, it will happen!*
And it did. Everything that I had felt, experienced, seen, written down and expected: it all fell into place when I had my personal reading with Judith, which we were able to arrange thanks to the

sister of my friend.

I had not often felt so seen, so understood and known. Mieke from the Essenes had already risen from her ashes. Now, much more and much older parts of my being came to the surface that were essential for me to be able to do what I have to do in this life. Many of which had been very difficult to bring into reality on Earth in former lives and they had had traumatic endings. But in this life, trust was able to be reinstalled with those higher parts of the Self.

Six months earlier, around Santa Claus time in December 2013, I had a reading with White Bull, through Ian Graham. He is a channeller and the author of *God Is Never Late, (But Never Early Either)*. I was reminded of his words.:
> "Many lives, you have lived in secret sacred societies. But now is the lifetime where you decide to come out of the closet. You can show yourself in your light, in your truth, in your celebration of Christ Love. Aha, your hour has come! You can start your ministry."

It touched something deep and primal within me to be acknowledged in the fact that I had lived many lives in hidden esoteric and mystic initiation schools having to do with Yeshua, Mary Magdalene and their heirs. My connection with them is deeply engraved in my whole being. This isn't something particularly special; it goes far beyond ego, identity or personal interests. It's about wanting to contribute to the raising of the consciousness of humankind, from my presence and mission, in tune with a greater good.

Suddenly, I understood my longstanding desperation at not being able to come into my own power because I didn't dare to give space to my deeper knowing. I had been denying the most divine parts of my essence and in doing so, surrendering to this remained unattainable.
My life entered an accelerated phase and I knew what I have to do; to walk this holy path, hand-in-hand with the Light World.

The Holy Grail, from a Pre-Raphaelites painting

By accessing this deep trust and understanding within myself I could now allow the presence and help from higher dimensions to come out with it. This is my personal report of my Journey to Love.

Crowning of the divine feminine

Before the Journey

It was completely clear to me. I had to go to the south of France. My feet needed to go and merge with the steps they had taken once before, a long time ago. And if there is such a clear inner knowing that you have to go because it serves a greater plan, it will be made possible, no matter what, right?

After having lived on 50 Euros a week for almost a year, in 2014, it seemed crazy to think that enough money would appear for me to go. But it did. My accountant gave me a letter that was all too welcome. I was very likely to receive money back from taxes and yes, it was a green light! I could really go!

Another confirmation also came through when my daughter Eva agreed to come with me. She is my daughter in this life, but when it comes to consciousness and high sensitivity, we are equals. We have visited sacred power places together before, including goddess sites and old sanctuaries in Glastonbury, Malta and Sicily.

We had soon discovered that we were soul sisters who knew each other thoroughly when deeply aligned. If there was a spiritual journey to be taken, she was the person for me to do it with!

Eva was due to go abroad for six months, from September 2015, for her studies in Brussels to another university of her choice, which was called going on Erasmus. Her first choice was Paris, a choice coming from the ambitious part in her. However, soon it became clear that the university in Paris wasn't welcoming Erasmus students that year. I smiled broadly when she told me that instead of going to Paris, it was 95 percent certain that she could go to Montpellier for the whole year. Montpellier! The perfect place to take off from to journeys in the south of France!

In the meantime, Judith Moore was back in our country and together we felt into the meaning of the trip. Soon it became clear to her what I had to do. "Work with the living Holy Grail and the activation of the Ark of the Covenant." This sounded a little vague to me at

25

Eva in France

that time, but soon I started to connect with it more and more and it began to land more deeply within me, often by going through several intense processes.

I received an initiation during that reading in a crystal chamber in the inner Earth, where I was told that I would be carefully prepared and guided to the places that would touch my Grail consciousness, through which I would be able to open up and remember even more. This turned out to be so true.

Grail Consciousness

What is the Holy Grail? You can read a hundred books about it and you probably still wouldn't have found a truly unambiguous answer. I've read a great deal about it myself. A lot of books and articles have been written in which thorough research has been conducted on the history and meaning of the Grail and the Ark of the Covenant. I'm not pretending to know the answer. To keep it as pure as possible, I can only tell you what resonates with me personally, coming from my wisdom, life experience and channel.

We all come from a Source in which Oneness, wisdom and love simply are. We will all return to that eventually. To draw a linear example: we all descended from the highest light, further and further away from our divinity.
This is why we slowly have forgotten that we are divine beings and we have identified more and more with the Earthly illusions and identities that we created within duality.
The deepest point in our long journey could be seen as the greatest, most traumatic human suffering, caused by destruction, desecration and the beastly eradication of certain human races. For many of us, this happened again during the Second World War. It can also go much further back, to the downfall of Atlantis. Both have caused a collective shock of consciousness, through which the consciousness process is re-activated in many people. The journey back to the remembering of who we are and where we came from started from experiencing the deepest point in the Earthly densification! The awakening starts in these unconscious, dark layers, where we had almost completely lost ourselves and our connection to the divine source.
To be able to grasp the immensity of our whole incarnation cycle, all we need to do is to tap into the help and guidance that is always available from the higher dimensions, and which, for simplicity, I call the Light World.

The Quest of the Holy Grail, Arthur Hughes

It is not our human me – often unconscious and still coming from self-interest – that decides the direction of our path. Our divine Self leads us with the utmost care, connected to guides, masters and/or angels from the Light World who stand by us during our process of awakening. If we can and wish to open up to this and we dare to trust and follow what is unfolding from the daily here and now, we follow the way of surrender to 'Thy Will be Done'.

I don't mean to say that we should put the responsibility for our lives outside ourselves and surrender ourselves like lame sheep to invisible forces! This pattern of submission wants to be over with as well; it is about time that we start to trust in our own wisdom again. Whether it is the church, a guru or another authority outside ourselves to which or whom we submitted; it served as practice material in duality. Seen from that perspective, it was part of the bigger plan.

This is what 'Thy Will Be Done' means for me: after getting to know and healing each split off part of our personality, we can reconnect again with our conscious Being. We allow ourselves to be guided by a higher will that serves the universal and divine law. To be able to experience this higher will, it is essential to start listening to the loving knowing of our hearts and travel our path from there. Whether this path goes to the left or to the right is immaterial; whatever path you take leads you to unity, wisdom, truth and love.

In many books about the Grail, the Holy Grail is spoken about as if it were an object. Some people argue that it could be the cup with which Joseph of Arimathea caught some of Yeshua's blood when he was hanging on the cross. Or the jug belonging to Mary Magdalene in which she kept essential oils and balms. Or a bowl or goblet with magical powers.

For me, the Holy Grail isn't a material thing. It's an Earthly coming together of the divine masculine and feminine powers of creation, like a uterus that receives, becomes pregnant, carries to term and gives birth. This is how Mary Magdalene received Yeshua and carried their children so they could convey their immaculate, divine DNA into the world.
I fully believe that in the ancient times, during the authentic Grail rituals, certain objects were used that carried a special energy, information or potency. These were charged with divine wisdom, knowledge and powers of creation only accessible to certain Grail priests. These people were acquainted with divine powers and knew how to use and handle them.

For most of us, this is still mostly way out of our reach. However, it does become interesting once we realise that these Grail stories are actually about us. The Holy Grail is a raised consciousness that goes far beyond the borders of our human, limited perception. For the most part, every human being who feels the calling can develop this consciousness.
Every occasion in our daily lives could be a reason to look beyond what has been presented as 'the truth' by the world around us up until now. When we are deeply touched by anything as human beings, there is an invitation to go within and seek out the deeper meaning of our existence in it.
Our body is a book in itself, containing all our old stories from multidimensional lives and flawlessly reacting to information that

The Vision of the Holy Grail, William Morris.

is important for our process of becoming conscious.

By listening attentively, while you are reading this book and by feeling what your body tells you, this allowing, feeling through, seeing through and transforming of the energetic messages that you receive could activate your Grail consciousness as well.

By now in our lives, we have played almost all available characters that are possible within Earthly duality, like those of the victim, perpetrator and saviour. This has led us towards a greater consciousness about what has been based on illusions or truth. We can free ourselves from the layers of judgement, guilt and pay-back; of drama, pain, fear, lovelessness, anger, sadness, poverty; and ignorance.

This is how an inner journey starts, one that will bring us back to our previous inner knowing that we are all divine creatures who live on the planet to learn from it; to be able to reach the full awakening of who we are in our deepest Essence.

All our potential for growth and the divine codes are already within our DNA. These are activated during every human crisis, large or small. When our personal healed layers are connected to our higher soul and divine layers, the activation of our Grail DNA is initiated. It is the descending of the pure light, which has only been able to stay alive in the world of the Spirit.

When we truly dare to get to know all the aspects of our personality and to see what they served, then we can fully integrate these different parts of ourselves and our fellow human beings. But now in a conscious way, into a much greater and unselfish love. This is how we become carriers of a higher, universal and divine knowing, of true divine love and wisdom. This is how we grow towards the living light of the Holy Grail and a Journey to Love.

♥

Sacré Coeur painting, Eglise (church) of Bugarach, France

History of the Grail

The fact that many people have gone before us in the quest for the Grail is shown by the many legends that exist. For example, Lancelot and Percival, the knights of the round table from the time of King Arthur. Or Floris and Blancheflour, a medieval Grail novel. But the history of the Grail actually goes back far beyond Yeshua. When we connect the Grail to the Ark, we arrive at Moses around 1450 BC.
I start with King David, born in 1040 BC. His descendants protected the Grail for centuries.

David's son Solomon built the first Temple in Jerusalem to guard and protect the Ark of the Covenant, which might have contained a Grail. Or, we could say, it was connected to Grail consciousness. The knowledge and wisdom, saved in documents, but also in crystals and objects, was passed through the descendants in these bloodlines. These were all carefully kept secret by their guards and protectors. Many of those descendants belonged to the highest initiates and were aiming for the complete embodiment of divine consciousness. This was the line that Yeshua was born into.

The Romans had been hunting down the guardians of the Grail (the ones who had knowledge of the Grail consciousness) before the arrival of Yeshua because they knew that those guardians had something that either they had to have themselves or that had to be eliminated. The gnostic and esoteric tradition, kept alive by the guardians of the Grail and that Yeshua secretly taught, was something that, in their eyes, conferred status and power.

Yeshua's proclamation with which he was trying to awake humanity; "Rise and remember yourself" was a thorn in the eye of the Romans and wasn't allowed in their growing empire and in their urge of expansion. Next to that there were (and still are!) hidden Earthly treasures of inestimable value. These consist of spiritual wealth that took on material form; they contribute to the raising of human consciousness. They hold divine powers. This is an important reason why carriers and protectors of the Grail have been hunted down for centuries, suppressed, tortured and wiped out.

Yeshua descends directly from King David, both from his father's and mother's sides.

He is thought to have died on the cross. But this is a story that the reformed Christian Church of Rome has completely turned around for their own behalf! By pointing to Yeshua as 'the Embodiment of God who rises above all people', by making us believe that he died on the cross, they made the path of the Grail a lot less accessible for 'simple souls like us, sinning and ignorant human beings.'

It becomes more and more clear how the Vatican hid or captured everything that could possibly remind humanity of its true origin.

We were told that we could only come to God if we kept to their edited commandments and prohibitions, giving away our power and surrendering like sheep to their authority which, to cap it all, also promises us salvation – especially by means of confession. This is how many of us lost the connection with, and the trust in, the pure divine teachings of Love.

After his possible crucifixion (where I feel he didn't die, but became present in another physical form, from a higher dimension of Light), or after whatever happened, he fled to Alexandria in Egypt to recover his strength. Later, he followed his wife Mary Magdalene to the Languedoc in the south of France. They were all accompanied by a part of their Holy Family and Essenes, many of whom carried the Grail consciousness. (If you would like to know more about this, read the Dead Sea Scrolls).

From the Languedoc the bloodlines would go on, amongst others through Joseph of Arimathea – who was a guardian of the Grail – to Avalon in Glastonbury and Scotland.

Together with 12 initiates he carried the Grail consciousness there. Several of them married local initiates to secure the pureness of the bloodlines in Great Britain. Other descendants stayed as guardians of the Ark, which was hosted in different places and had to be

Venez à moi, vous tous qui souffrez, qui êtes accablés et je vous soulagerai
(Come to me, all of you who suffer, who are overwhelmed and I will relieve you)
Sculpture in the church of Rennes-le-Château, France

moved as soon as the 'wrong people' got wind of it. Rennes-le-Château might well have hosted the Ark for some time in a Visigoth fortress.

Many Cathars lived in the south of France in medieval times. They carried out an important role in this history. Many of us are reincarnated Cathars and these Cathars were often reincarnated Essenes! They lived the secret teachings of Yeshua and Mary Magdalene, the authentic esoteric traditions and gnosis. It is very likely that they possessed documents that contained the original words of Yeshua and Mary Magdalene. They inspired people to take their own responsibility and to "Rise up and remember yourself". They absolutely didn't believe in salvation from without. In complete simplicity they lived their Journey to Love.

Several Cathars were members of the Order of the Knights Templar – or the other way around - and this is how the ancient knowledge has been protected and embodied through time.

In the south of France, there were many Cathar fortresses and more hidden places in which they could protect themselves. Montségur was a very important one. But during the Albigensian Crusades that started in 1209, almost all of the Cathars who didn't want to

Travellers at the Cathar Castle of Montségur, an old image in the village of Montségur, France

surrender to the then already corrupted Christianity were killed.

The Cathars at Montségur didn't want to renounce their beliefs. In 1244 they voluntarily walked into the fire singing, trusting that they would be received directly into the divine light.

The Templars also played a big role in the history of the Grail. This Order of Knights from the 12th century was set up to protect and ensure the existence of the descendants of the Holy Family. In their time, they consisted mainly of the royal descendants of the Merovingians. Next to that, they guarded the Ark of the Covenant and the Holy Grail. It's highly likely that they took the Ark, together with many material treasures, from Ethiopia to the south of France. Because of the high number of raids and ransacking, they had to look again and again for shelter for the holy objects that were in their care. Some things were brought to the North of Spain (Catalonia, Pyrenees), to Portugal and to Scotland, including a hidden space beneath the Rosslyn Chapel, which is by the way an exact copy of the Temple of Solomon in Jerusalem.

After the murder, elimination or flight of almost all Templars, many of their treasures and rituals were taken over by the Order of Freemasonry.

It is beautiful to see that in many Marian churches, often built on old

Priestess with Templar Chalice, Eglise (church) de Rennes-le-Chateau, France

sanctuaries, old symbols and codes were left that directly pointed to these Orders of Knights. And they in turn point to ancient knowledge on the process of becoming spiritually conscious.

37

During the Second World War the Grail was hunted down by Hitler and Himmler. They had a lot of knowledge and set up an order of Nazi – Neo Templars with a circle of initiates, believing that they could create a certain 'pure race' with the Ubermensch. They even sent Otto Rahn, who was an expert concerning the spiritual knowledge and heritage of the Cathars, to the south of France, with the mission to acquire the Grail. They also wanted to take over the holy entries to the Light network of the Earth, like they tried to do in the Externsteine in Germany. Himmler confirmed this as a holy place for the Nazis.

We all know and remember how inhumane the desecration of the Second World War was, coming from a domination and regime that was purely based on lust for power, fear and destruction. Through the centuries many sacred power places that used to embody both the masculine and feminine in perfect balance have been exploited and contaminated by the intrusion of dark forces. The ruling masculine has completely dominated, disempowered and locked up the receptive feminine.

Knowing that this was all part of the Divine plan and necessary to be able to reach complete self-knowledge, these holy places can now be lovingly opened and restored with our consciousness. This means that the old, original divine energy can flow again freely through the Light network of the Earth, which will rise the frequency in that area and will uplift our collective fields.
This is a part of the Light Work that I conducted during my trip in the south of France in 2015. Alongside that I'm dedicated to the guiding of my fellow travellers on their sincere, holy quest and their Journey to Love.

Off to the Second Holy Land

During my preparations at home, I delved into the history of the Languedoc. I had heard many enthusiastic stories about it, but I wanted to stay true to my own observations. On the internet I researched Mary Magdalene in France and this was how I got to know the book(s) of Jaap Rameijer. He was the co-owner of Les Labadous, the place to stay for every spiritual lover of this area who wanted to spend time in the paradise of higher dimensions surrounding Rennes-le-Chateau in France.

I also started looking for people who, from what I felt, had a pure connection with the ancient knowledge that is so tangible in that area. A new but very familiar world opened up for me; of the Holy Family, Druids, Essenes, Merovingians, Cathars, Templars and Freemasons. Every time I added another piece to what could become the contents of my journey, every part of the authentic esoteric and mystical knowledge that I could re-activate through my own essence, I knew that I would be able to pass on and activate in other people.

While part of me was already 'there', a flow suddenly started up and my channel was opening more and more. After a year of intensive processing, I sometimes wondered whether I was reaching the limit of it all still being bearable. At times I felt so extremely open that I had to turn around on my bike when I was half-way to the centre of Zutphen from my home, because I couldn't bear the commotion of the town.

However, as my dear like-minded friend Marianne often stated, 'It's no longer about being comfortable or not being comfortable. It's about being with what is present'.
A golden quote that made me sit on the couch with bowed head over and over again, being with what was moving inside of me.

Often, this surrender led to precious moments. I can't stress enough how immense and loving the invitation of the Light World is to tune into them. They have so much to offer us, so much to give. Often a part of our personality is in the way and sometimes literally stands between our 'I here' and 'Divine Self there'. Sabotaging this connection means that we are giving in to our ego and keeping ourselves unwillingly imprisoned in the lower dimensions, where duality rules.

I have met many of my inner saboteurs. Some have been dismantled and 'melted down' by love, others require permanent clarity and a deeper surrender to what wants to guide me to 'the real me'. Some carry very old, negative self-images that are very hard to let go of. Getting stuck in their energy and illusions is like being captured in survival mode again, which is based on fear. The only way out is by allowing Love and Light to touch their wounded parts, to find a way out of these old restricted fields. Believe me: behind the veils they have a much better sat nav for that than we can ever imagine here in our three-dimensional world!

A Loving Visit

I tried to surrender as much as possible to what wanted to happen each day. During one of those days, I was sitting on the couch. I had suffered a sleepless night in which it became clear that my old 'me' was still trying to diminish the transmissions that I received, while I very much appreciated them from a higher perspective. Feeling into this, I received an email from another friend. Her frustration about the fact that her connection with the Light World seemed to decrease (while she was indirectly witnessing my connection only becoming stronger every day) was becoming more and more unbearable. I recognized this myself and know that this is the case for everyone who is about to truly surrender to higher guidance.
I'd like to share my messages and notes about what information I was inwardly receiving at that moment.

I'm completely involved in a process myself. Now that I've emailed you, the boiling waters come to a rest a little. I think I understand your feeling of being in two worlds. Please email me if you want to share more about this. It might be superfluous to tell you this, but it could anchor things. I will also turn inwards myself, align, and at the right moment I will also tune into you.

***

Bingo, straight away. I'm sitting on the couch. My heart is about to explode out of my chest, I'm sobbing deeply and immediately feel the energy of Yeshua and Mary Magdalene next to me.

***

I never before received so much information at once. I became dizzy and heard that my frequency is increasing daily, so as to be able to connect to the right dimensions. I saw the eyes and hands of Yeshua. So soft and full of love. He told me "You can't give up now. Stay faithful to your heart".

41

I asked why it had to be this way. He showed me how I'm being stimulated right now to turn to the highest and purest truth over and over again. My inner light grows so much by doing this that I can even go beyond trust; trust becomes knowing. I feel Mary Magdalene's energy next to me, she's here to encourage me. She shows me how she, too, sometimes became desperate, and how this strengthened her.

Mary Magdalene arrives on land in the south of France and is welcomed by a Nazarene Priestess. Painting in the Eglise (church) of St. Salvayre, France

I saw someone coming, appearing from the mists. Joseph of Arimathea. He had little dimples in his cheeks, a very sympathetic charisma. They assured me that I would be guided on this journey, at an easy pace. The Grail would become even clearer to me. There, in France, the original contents of the Ark of the Covenant aren't present physically. However, the codes, the knowledge, and an etheric crystal of divine creation forces, are.

***

"In the meantime, your friend is being prepared to become acquainted with these layers within herself and to remember how it is to feel that she's carried at every step towards the complete unfolding of the plan that is captured within her DNA."

***

At the time, I become conscious of a voice that was obviously directed to my friend.

Dear Soul Sister

The daily burdens will always be there in the Earthly dimensions. We understand that this is sometimes weighing down heavily on you. We know this burden too; like a never-ending threat she was always present in the background and sometimes unavoidably close. But don't let this discourage you!
In essence, she's a loving invitation to come closer to yourself. Even though this is very hard to acknowledge, this is how it is. There is nothing but divinity. The fact that this seems to keep coming back on your path means that in her highest appearance it is pointing towards the finer divine layers within yourself. We could handle it by discovering the balance within ourselves, by tending to what kept us in connection with our Creator.
The challenge for you is to start to value yourself, so you can discover the same divine balance and guard it. If you want to contact your Creator, first make contact with the part in you where love dwells. This is how you free up the way to any dimension. Don't deny the emotions that fester within you about the threat of the Earthly separation, which in reality keeps you away from your light.

See her as the entrance into your truth. Your emotion of anger is an old one, like a door you can open to a truthful part of yourself that is longing for reunion with the divine. Know that there will always be someone to receive you, if you find the courage to follow the impulses that come from within your Soul. Passionately long for a new balance, create the balance and the path that you are looking for will unfold beneath your feet.

A few hours after receiving this message I went to bed, feeling impressed that everything felt so close. The guidance was almost tangible and the loving truth was given to us so effortlessly. It felt almost 'too good to be true'.

On our way to the Holy Land at Rennes-le-Château

What a rich feeling it was! And now, the journey was about to begin.
The practical things had been arranged; the flight was booked;
the B&Bs reserved; and my daughter, who would travel with me
as a soul sister on this spiritual quest, was informed sufficiently to
know what we were about to do. Off we go to Montpellier first, to
get to know her new study and living quarters for the next year.
After that, we are off to the second Holy Land, as the Languedoc is
rightly called.

I would be able to feel these old beloved lands, without really knowing 'what' to feel. I knew that in some places where I had lived several lives – not always light lives seen from the human point of view - the hidden holy knowledge has been kept upright like a token of light. Oh … I couldn't wait to go.

Departure

At the train station in Zutphen, I feel tired and a little emotional. I'm looking forward to diving into myself on the train. At the same time, I realise that Eva has started her last final test of this school year. What a synchronicity again! We are both doing some kind of test of competence; me after a long education of many lifetimes; and how exciting; the Lightworker within me can start to do her work again!

I'm aware of my own inner masculine, who arranged everything perfectly back home even though a sleepless night had preceded it; the one who took my suitcase up the stairs in the railway station and who is comforting me now. "Don't worry, it will all go without any effort. You will see. Just relax."

I am off to the south of France! Today, my journey goes to Belgium, to get closer to the Charleroi Airport, from where we will take off tomorrow.

Incognito on the train to Charleroi Airport, Belgium

The train has been going for almost three hours now, with a slightly tired version of me in it, after a night in which I lay awake a lot, feeling even more layers opening.

My heavy walking shoes and lower legs rest on my suitcase and I'm staring out of the window. I realise I don't look like a Lightworker at all.

The first call to go within comes when we have crossed the Belgium border and the train stops at a little railway station with the name Kijkuit, which means Watch Out! At first, I take this as a warning. Then, I realise this is a fear-based interpretation and that is not what this journey is about! So, I plug into the name again and I hear, *Why don't you put out your watchers.* Oh yes, of course and I immediately close my eyes.

Straight away I'm being taken into a hilly landscape, like I'm going for a walk in it. What is that in the distance? I hold my breath and look. Tears come to my eyes. My brothers and sisters are waiting for me there! Some wave with white rags as a loving welcome. My attention is pulled towards the right, a beautiful child of colour is sitting there, looking at me with a very wise expression. I connect with her, she comes running towards me and when I see her up close, I feel that we know each other.

"I'm Arrara," she says. While we embrace each other, everything falls into place. This is my holy family, and the beautiful child that I feel is my current daughter Eva in one of her previous lives. Wow, this is such a beautiful welcome home.

And I am only in Kijkuit!

Four hours later, I'm sitting with a freshly-washed face with a nice cool beer and a bowl of tasty olives in a colourful Italian Restaurant in a strange and bleak suburb of Charleroi. I'm so happy that I made this journey today and that I don't have to do this tomorrow before catching the flight! I thought the airport would be close to the railway station where I arrived, but that wasn't the case at all.

It started off with the journey to the unfamiliar railway station of Charleroi Sud. I haven't often seen so many construction sites as on the way between Brussels and my final stop. It was such a contrast, all this material rubble, in comparison to the clean and green environment where I live, let alone where I was about to go to! Fortunately, the train was long so my compartment was quiet; I could still breathe.

A few stops before Charleroi, a rough, enormous and pompous looking guy in a contrasting very smart suit stepped into train. He was too remarkable not to notice:
a skin of colour; pitch-black sunglasses; and a rasta look, all on top of a very smart looking, bright white shirt. When we got off the train in Charleroi, he asked me in French that was so fluent whether I needed help with my suitcase. I was thinking about what he actually said and smiled. Before I could pronounce the correct French words, he had already taken off with my suitcase.

This was going a little too fast. I ran after him. He didn't take any notice of me, he went straight down the packed staircase with my big heavy suitcase, which looked more like a handbag in his hands. While I was trying not to lose him, I thought *either someone sent me an angel and this is part of the journey, or I really need to be cautious right now* .... Once down the stairs, in the midst of so many people and hallways, he looked back and started off on another French sentence. Without letting him finish I called out to him.
"Merci beaucoup, ça va comme ça!" (Thank you so much, it's fine like this!)
He looked at me through his dark sunglasses, smiled, put down my suitcase and off he went. *Brave girl,* I said to myself. There I was, in the middle of the tunnel. I had no idea where to go. I started to take off following my intuition. Within three minutes, I was outside the railway station in front of an Ibis hotel. *Ah, so my hotel must be close then, too,* I thought. This wasn't the case either, explained a helpful Belgium lady in halting English. I had to take the bus to the aeroport, she told me.

This went well and twenty minutes later I arrived at Brussels, Charleroi Airport. According to the hotel voucher there were shuttle buses to take me to the hotel for free. But I didn't see them.
However, I did discover what the bus for the airport looked like.

Charleroi Flight

That was good to know, because Eva would arrive here the following day by bus. After calling the hotel, the owner came to pick me up after fifteen minutes. And after another fifteen minutes, I lay down on the first guest bed of this beautiful journey full of surprises!

♥

PART TWO:

The South of France

The delightful Mediterranean atmosphere in Montpellier

We Start off on Earth

After taking Eva into my arms at the airport everything seems to become a daze. We had both been looking forward to this moment so much and now that it was finally there, we had to remind each other that it was really happening. The flight was fast and here we were ... outside the Montpellier Airport, where my eye fell on an Occitan Cross. I feel goosebumps straight away, *Yes, we are really diving into it now...*

For Eva this will be a special journey too because she was becoming aware of a Cathar life that had been very essential for her. This might be touched and opened up again during our journey. Full of expectation we walked into the south of France.
After searching we find a comfortable shuttle bus that would take us to the centre of the town. Before we finally take off, we were waiting for at least 45 minutes until literally nobody else could fit in the bus. During the wait, we studied the map with bus and tram connections and we saw many young people. Probably students, like Eva and then we felt the energy of Montpellier.

In the centre of the town, we start off on a discovery while we still have our luggage with us. Not my strongest side; I don't like dragging around a heavy suitcase with a badly shaped handle in my sensitive hands. But we are hungry and we want to eat in a nice place. We end up on what turns out to be the largest and most popular terrace square in Montpellier. The city looks beautiful! The daylight seems to be much cleaner and nourishing than in the Netherlands. As far as this is possible in a big city, there is a cosy atmosphere that makes our food taste even better.

After that we drag our luggage back, looking for a tram that will take us closer to our B&B. This is rather easy; it looks like Eva already knows the way.

Half an hour later, I ring the doorbell next to a gate behind where our B&B should be, with a sigh of relief. Zelda, a beautiful, young Jewish looking woman opens the door. She touches me immediately and in hindsight I hear that Eva had the same experience. With a broad smile Zelda welcomes us and she leads us through her garden to the charming house. The name of the B&B is already promising, *Havre de Paix*; meaning Haven of Peace; and it truly was a peaceful place in a busy city.

After a more practical guided tour around the house, we get a passionate tour around the garden. Zelda keeps an organic garden and I feel the fire of an Indigo-being in her; she puts her heart and soul into creating a better world. Later, after we went inside because of the mosquitoes, she says she trusts us because our auras feel good. We have her house to ourselves this weekend. She reminds me of our Jewish ancestors and I'm wondering internally whether this is why she touches me.

We retreat to our rooms, kick off our big hiking shoes that are way too warm and plop down on the large bed. After a little rest, a shower rinses off the dust of the journey. The map of Montpellier shows that Eva's student residence is indeed only one tram stop from our B&B. We passed it on the tram and it looked promising!

Too tired to do anything else, we make our plans for the next day. Sitting down at Zelda's big table she's showing us the nicest way to the centre – which turns out to pass by Eva's new room – and a good organic shop. Zelda will not cook for us, so that's our first task for the next day: buying healthy food.

Growing Roots in Montpellier

Our Dutch rice-crackers and spelt-bread fall well into our empty stomachs. With new energy we head off into town, with money, a map and a bottle of water in our bags. Walking in the direction that Zelda showed us there are impressive arcade arches in the distance. It turns out the arches continue to stretch out over a long distance, as one long impressive monument which is pointing towards the centre. Unexpectedly, we end up on the doorstep of Eva's new residence for the year, right next to this monument. Again, what a special place… Almost all the windows have been blinded; the building seems deserted. Apparently, the summer holidays had already begun?

We can't see which is the front or back door so we explore the enormous building complex. While I'm 'checking' inwardly whether

Eva in front of her new Cité Universitaire in Montpellier

we are in line with the bigger plan and Eva is checking another wall for an entrance and a large metal gate, that seemed motionless before, suddenly opens. Two chatting girls walk out and Eva sneaks in, with a straight face, as if she's been studying there for years. I follow her and realise that it's not a coincidence that this door opens for her.

And just like that we are in the middle of her new student residence. There is a panel with a map and we decide to go to the reception after all, to register Eva as a new student for the coming year. Someone's giving us permission to look around.

"However," the lady of the reception says, "You can't enter the buildings, because officially it's the summer-holidays." *We'll see about that,* we think.

Sometimes bravery suddenly occurs, without knowing where it comes from. While we walk up the stairs towards the front door of a building, Eva pushes the door with and "Open Sesame", it opens. Wow, what an impressive lobby … We randomly walk up more stairs and we enter a floor where, on both sides of the hallway, there are small rooms. The cleaners are working there and they are friendly, they answer all our questions and allow us to look around. Eva's building - for Erasmus-students - turns out to be a little further away.

Later, we leave this building and we walk around her building with our cameras. Such a nice atmosphere! Mediterranean and sunny. Exploring as much as we can we are mesmerized. Eva takes a moment getting herself used to the place and then we walk out of the complex through a back door that is electronically guarded. We come out in the middle of the centre of Montpellier. Like Zelda said, we find an organic shop a little further down the road. But the coffee-bar that we're standing right next to appeals to me more and we decide to have a coffee first. We order a lovely cappuccino.

When I discover two broomsticks that are standing next to a tree, something awakens in me … I can't hold myself back and put one between my legs. "See you later alligator," I say. At that moment another woman comes in for a coffee, looks at us and offers to take a picture. Yes, our liberating adventure has really begun!

Who knows, I might still be able to do it?

What a care-free life and we still have so many days to go! After our coffee we discover the organic shop and oh, this is such a good start of our holidays. We are meeting only nice people, we buy honest products, and we have all the time in the world. We can totally see

Eva going here for her shopping with her little student bag!
After a picnic lunch in Zelda's home, we're off again. Eva's university is somewhere at the other side of the centre and of course we'd like to discover that too.
The afternoon is long. Very long. We walk and walk, for hours, on our trustworthy Teva-sandals, but it can't be prevented that we both

La fontaine des Trois Grâces, Montpellier

get blisters on our feet. There's no end to the charming alleys and endless zigzagging streets with shops and terraces.

We head into a pharmacy to buy toothpicks and blister-bandages. We discover a bookstore with five floors - to lose yourself in - with a gigantic selection of books with of course many books about the Cathars, Templars, Languedoc, etc. They also sell stuff for painting which is great, if Eva might get into a painting mood again. We resist, realising that whatever we buy now, we will have to take home in our already heavy suitcases. We buy a map of Montpellier and a roadmap of the Languedoc, so we'll be able to find the way to our lodging addresses, once we get our rental car on Sunday.

Suddenly we've had it. I feel that I start to go into survival mode. My mood starts to decrease and this means for me that I should look for quiet and silence. Eva says she's hungry. But finding a peaceful and quiet terrace with good food in such a busy city is easier said than done. After an hour we still haven't found anything. We decide to start walking towards the tram stop. This doesn't turn out to be a good plan; we end up in a rather cheerless looking neighbourhood. But we've walked this far now and we're already way over our limits anyway. After more than six hours of walking those extra 15 minutes don't really matter anymore. I'm walking squint already to try to avoid my blisters. And then … totally unexpectedly, in a bleak corner, we discover some sort of entry in an old wall, through which there is a most beautiful little square with inviting terraces. Delighted, we sit down on the wooden chairs and see that there are lots of tasty dishes on the menu. Fortunately, we hadn't given up and we didn't end up on a nasty terrace in the midst of loads of tourists. After a nourishing meal and a glass of delicious white wine, we're off to the tram stop. It gets a little tense because we don't have a ticket yet and the tram is about to arrive, but it turns out that I have enough coins for the ticket machine and our tram tickets fly out of the machine exactly on time. Lucky again.

Two stops later, a big and very colourful a band gets in. The musicians are all dressed in red and looking very festive. They soon start playing a catchy tune, which makes face after face light up in the tram. What an amusing ending of a physically challenging, but also definitely very enriching day!

At our arrival home we have a wonderful meeting with Zelda, who turns out to be half Polish and half Moroccan. She is Jewish, through her Polish mother. I tell her that I carry Jewish blood as well, through a Polish great-grandmother whose bloodline goes back to the south of France. Carefully, I suggest that we might already know each other from a former life: "If you ask me, we're old acquaintances."
Aromatherapy, spirituality, Jewish blood, world culture and the inner drive to make the world more beautiful; we got along immediately and it almost feels obvious to be so trusting and not needing many words together. She looks at me with her dark eyes and I wonder what this meeting means to her.

A little later Eva and I are lying on our beds, to allow space for all the impressions we have received. I'm glad we planned this at the beginning of our journey, so we can go inwards after this. The blisters are also telling us to have some rest and I know it is time to align myself and surrender.
The next morning, we start off with a beautiful moment with Zelda. She couldn't let go of what I had said yesterday and when we tune in, I share what comes up. I can see her becoming softer and more accessible with every sentence I say. We are all touched by how this meeting feels arranged for us. This contact might come in handy later on.
One hour later, we decide to go into the centre again, now that we are still here. When we leave Montpellier tomorrow, we won't be back here until Eva will start her adventure as an Erasmus-student. After another morning of enjoying the lively and cosy city, exploring and getting to know it, we feel as if we have had enough around lunch time. So, we return and it is wonderful to be back in the *Havre de Paix* and to be able to process all the impressions we have already taken in since the beginning of this journey. To start off with thought, we don't really feel like relaxing because we are so full of all we have seen and experienced. Later in the day we start to feel a little slower.

'Oranje boven' (a Dutch exclamation which means as much as 'Orange above all')
– Damien brings us to Carcassonne with his VW van

When we want to book our tickets for the train from Montpellier to Carcassonne, Eva suddenly remembers that we can also look at the website of blablacar.com and try to get a ride with a private driver. Well, it turns out there are four rides listed, so we can choose.

We discover Damien, who still has two spots left in his cosy van. His departure time is an hour later than we need, which will mean we won't make it in time for our rental car in Carcassonne. We click on his profile anyway and what do we see? He just posted a message that he will leave an hour earlier. It's all being wonderfully arranged for us!
With a grateful heart we pack our suitcases, cook a nice organic dinner, before we dive into our beds early. Probably we've had the most Earthly part of our journey now …

B&B Les Marguerites in Alet-les-Bains

Following the Ark

After a comfortable ride on two trams through town we are picked up by Damien, who is waving to us exuberantly from his jolly orange VW van. There is enough space left for us and our luggage. What an angel. There is such a light-hearted, cosy atmosphere in the roaring, fully packed van. He is helping a friend to move and has a lot of stuff in his van. He is also from the area but he doesn't know that much about the Cathars or Templars. It is kind of sobering to realise that not everyone who lives here, shares this knowledge.

Damien does know that the roads in the area where we want to go are very bendy, hilly and narrow and you have to drive carefully. When he says this, my stomach starts to tense up. I have never before rented a car or driven in another country besides the Netherlands, let alone driven through the mountains. One of my fears is being triggered here. I try to comfort myself inwardly with words like; *This journey is meant to be, it is so guided. I'm sure you're not meant to drive off a cliff!* I direct my attention back to the carefree cosiness in the orange van and realise that a Holy Land is waiting for us.

After fully insuring our rental car – just in case - at the rental place at the airport in Carcassonne, we let out a deep sigh of relief and put our luggage in it. Thank God, no more dragging around of suitcases and bags. Once we're on the road, I feel my excitement. It is a magical, powerful and touching feeling to put my foot on the gas and drive off towards the area where my heart has felt so at home for so many lifetimes.

Within no time we have lunch in an old and picturesque square in Limoux and soon after that we enter Alet-les-Bains. On the way we feel the frequency rising. Wow, such a high energy here …

We both feel dizzy when we get out of the car. With open arms we are received by Antoinette, at her beautiful B&B, Les Marguerites. This is an extract from my diary that afternoon.

Wow ... here we are, in heavenly Alet-les-Bains, in the most luxurious B&B ever. If it wouldn't have been for Judith Moore's advice that this was the best place to stay, I would have never booked this place for 85 Euros per night. But, let's get this straight: the poverty-consciousness is over! I allow myself some luxury, so the energy that I need to do what I'm here for is available at all times. I surround myself with loving atmospheres that keep reminding me that I have started a new episode in this Earthly adventure! This is a completion of duality, also in the sense of expensive or cheap. I'm tuning into receiving and enjoying, flowing in and flowing out. A higher plan wants to be served.

It is written that the Ark of the Covenant has been hidden here in a castle, up on a mountain. I will ask the warm-hearted host and hostess whether they know which mountain that might have been. All that is left of the castle are a few stones; we'll have to investigate the mountains first.

My intestines start working again too. I think the crystal energy within me with which I took off from home, had to be protected. So, I armoured myself in the big city. But here, I make contact with the mountain tops across from where we are staying. And the energy starts to work within me now and it feels like I can open up more already.

In Alet-les-Bains

After installing ourselves in our room we are ready for our first intuitive walk through Alet in the end of the afternoon. While we looking around, we feel as if we are stepping into a different time, my eye falls on a door with a poster on it. It looks strange; this modern A4 2015 poster on such an old house. I read; Nicolas de Leon, for guides etc. and I realise how much I enjoy following my nose; here is a guide already!

We walk further and pass an old city gate. I suddenly hear, *Stop, just stop.* I don't understand why, I don't see anything special … so we decide to continue. When we reach a larger building, my body suddenly stops. It turns out to be the backside of a building that I wanted to visit, Lorrie's Angels Gallery.

I have seen Lorrie's Gallery on Facebook several times, with beautiful angels and inspiring sculptures. However, it is closed now; it's already past six o'clock. We walk on and enjoy the pleasant fairy-tale like atmosphere along the River Aude. In a back alley we discover an old, but renovated restaurant. How interesting; it is the former garden of the old seminary.

"Until the 16th century devout young men were educated here," says the friendly man who stuffs our table with Earthly delights. "After that, until the 20th century, it was some kind of religious schooling centre for women." My intuition tells me that this was a place of the secret passing on of ancient knowledge for centuries.

We are sitting across from the old ruined Abbey, which was inhabited by monks who were protected by Templars for a long time. With full bellies, we thank the friendly owner of the restaurant and cross the street towards the Abbey.

The remains are impressive, but don't give me any other experiences. We are the only visitors apart from a young guy who is franticly taking pictures.

The ruined Abbey in Alet-les-Bains

Apparently, I'm in his way, when he puts one of his feet on the small stone on which both of my feet are as well and I get out of his way. "Is taking pictures your hobby, or do you have a special reason?" I ask him.

He enthusiastically tells me that he is an independent photographer and a while ago, in a tourist office in Carcassonne, he saw some folders about Alet-les-Bains that were completely outdated and not attractive at all in his eyes.

He suggested to make them a new folder and that's how he got a deal.

Then, I carefully inquire if he knows anything about the mountain which has the ruin of the castle, of which has been said that it temporarily hid the Ark of the Covenant. He looks at me as if I asked the weirdest question ever. After an obvious silence, he answers: "There is only a ruined Abbey here, nothing else."

Ha,ha, you don't fool me, goes through my head ...

In silence, a little tired from the day, Eva and I walk back to our B&B. I can't yet picture our plan for tomorrow, so I decide to let it rest in the hands of the gods and go to bed.

Taken by the hand

While we are having our first breakfast in the beautiful garden, we feel that it is already too hot to climb a mountain in the sun. While Antoinette is giving us delicacies, I ask her how she got here. A wise woman starts to talk. She had been thinking about getting back into a Jewish Community, by marrying her loved one in Israel. However, 'fortunately' she didn't follow through with this because she had already done so in a former life. It was clear to her that she and her husband had to be guardians of a healing place here in Alet. So that was and it is still her calling …

This place feels very clean and protected and lies in the middle of several healing sources. Eva and I feel very lucky to start our Grail journey here. When Antoinette returns with fresh coffee, I ask her what arises in her about what we could do today. She sums up several touristic spots, but I don't feel any resonance. I tell her something about our spiritual quest, which changes things.

She tells us that we definitely should visit the little church in St. Salvayre, which we can reach by taking a small road from the middle of the village. Then, she talks about a Spanish Jew who knows everything about the Essenes who lived in Alet around the time of Yeshua and Mary Magdalene.

We both get goosebumps when she says this. *This is it!* When she tells us his name, I feel the Light World smiling: Nicolas de Leon. That was the name on the strange poster on the old house! Antoinette will give Nicolas a call; we'll await the response and it will become apparent whether it's truly meant to be that we meet this person and whether he's up for a talk.

However, she's not able to reach Nicolas at this moment. Apparently, he has some physical problems and he's not the first to get up in the morning. Eva and I decide to walk off into the village. If Nicolas isn't at home, we will start with a meditation and alignment in the ruined Abbey or the church next to it.

Half an hour later, we're standing in front of Nicolas' house. No

The Goddess Minerva/Diana, Alet-les-Bains village

response. I try the number on the poster again but get the answering machine. In a few French sentences I haphazardly try to explain that we are interested in the Essene lives that have been lived here. Eva is impressed. Proudly, she looks at me and that makes me trust that whatever is on his answering machine will be comprehensible. That's all we can do in that moment, so we walk back towards the church. After about ten steps, a car passes and Eva jokingly says: "That might just be Nicolas!"

Excitement gets hold on me while he passes by, so I decide to follow the car. He goes out of sight but I keep on going. And when I reach the parking spot behind the city walls, I see a man slowly getting out of his car. He does look like a Spanish Jew, I think. It must be him. Once he is standing up, I see two friendly eyes above a large cigar.

"Nicolas?" I ask.

A little later, we find ourselves in a small stuffy room and are warmly invited to join him at the kitchen table. The remains of his breakfast show that we've stepped into his life unexpectedly. But we're here to discover who Nicolas is and what he has in store for us. He is very sympathetic and starts to elaborate on how we've been fooled by the church for centuries. I might only be able to understand a quarter of what he is saying, but he is so verbose that more than enough of value remains. During his long story I can feel Eva drifting away. I start to interrupt him more frequently because I too have difficulties in keeping up with what he is very passionately, telling us.

A small doubt arises about the value of this meeting, all of which makes me a little bit impatient in listening as well. Out of the blue I start talking about the Essenes intending to make it clear to him why we are here – if necessary, figuratively by means of gesticulations.

"D'accord, oui," he says, "oui, je comprends." (Yes, I agree, oh yes, I understand.)

But he wants to make it clear where all this is leading. After a few more sentences I understand that St. Salvayre is a very special place that we should visit and he mentions something about tectonic plates and sacred old menhirs. He talks about "Les menhirs qui parlent" (The menhirs who speak) that have been placed on the fault lines of the Earth with a special meaning.

"You can tap on them, not forcefully, but softly. You will feel how the stone resonate," he says, while he shows with his hands how we should do this. I understand that this is something we can find at St. Salvayre. Years later, when I speak him again about this book,

71

Looking for Roubichoux with Nicolas de Leon

it turns out he meant the menhirs in the field, not the one in the church!

Suddenly he gets up, picks up a piece of paper, writes something on it while murmuring away, then walks across to his huge screen and starts looking for something. In a scrawl I see him noting Roubichoux. He's got a hit. I can feel it.

"There was an Essene sanctuary there in the first century. When they restored the church they found big pieces of stone, with Aramaic inscriptions."

I hold my breath while he continues; he doesn't know that I lived here in this environment in the first century. Smiling, he continues. "I don't know why I'm telling you this now, it's probably my intuition. It seems to work sometimes."

While he is looking for a map online that shows Roubichoux, he tries to clarify how to get there. There is a website that mentions Roubichoux but it doesn't give directions. He mentions Chalabre and another village; it should be "Somewhere around there".

That is remarkable … A few days before my departure to France a friend of mine was very touched by an image of a Templar's armour.

She couldn't let it go and a few days later she found out that the armour was to be found in Chalabre …

After a good hour we are back outside. I have two bits of paper with some notes scribbled down. Nicolas had really made an effort for us! Eva and I tried very hard to understand his French and make the most of all he wanted to tell us. We both feel the need to go back to our rooms first to freshen up a little. We yawn, shower and fan ourselves intensively in the garden with Antoinette's beautiful lavender plants. They help us to ground and integrate all that we are able to receive.

Quite some time later we get into our rental car. I say a quick prayer that the mountain track won't be too steep and we take the exit towards St. Salvayre.

We are zigzagging about three miles up and then we see a small church on a corner.

This must be it! The car can cool down in the shade behind a large ramshackle barn. While I reach out with my feelers and slowly walk into the church, Eva has already found the menhir and sits down next to it. We both experience a special balance of masculine and feminine energy in this place. It feels remarkably clean and harmonious. Eva starts to feel heavy; she sits with her hand on the pillar, in silence, softly tapping the stone. After a while, she looks at me a little disappointed and says, "I don't feel anything".

The little church from the 12ᵗʰ century in St. Salvayre

73

She continues to tap for a little longer, while I'm walking around taking pictures and I feel a very peaceful silence arising. A little later, I sit down next to Eva. I can embrace the pillar with my lower legs. It is definitely a seriously masculine menhir. At first, I'm being sucked into the earth like lead and before I realise what is happening, I end up in hidden civilizations. My spine seems to become the same sort of pillar as the one I'm touching. I close my eyes, ground myself and feel how I start to rise up from the church. I end up in a transparent Lemurian atmosphere where there is only silence and eternity.

In the meantime, Eva is taking pictures that are far better than what is possible with my mobile phone. Later on, we almost fall over laughing at a picture in which I do, in fact, look like a vague, long and transparent being that is being sucked into the universe.

When I feel at one with the pillar, I softly tap it with my right hand. And yes indeed: my left hand is receiving signals. The stone 'answers.' I get the hang of it and feel how, very subtly, every one of my touches is being answered with the same intention. There is clearly a connection. It is very special …

When we have both felt enough, we walk down the road in silence, out of the village. There are two men on the street and they greet us sympathetically. It is remarkable how warm and welcoming everyone is; nobody looks at us with eyes like; "Oh look, there go a

Interior of the little church in St. Salvayre

74

Hostelry l'Eveché, Alet-les-Bains

few strange tourists". After we have enjoyed the view and filled our lungs full of fresh mountain air, we walk back to our car. It is such a luxury to have the car available to us every day!

When we are back down in Alet, we're hungry and decide to go into the more up-market restaurant l'Evêché. It is quite expensive, but then we are used to low-budget holidays and nothing else is open today. It is a beautiful hostelry in the old episcopal Palace dating from the 12th century. It was also part of the Abbey and is situated in the middle of the green, peaceful area along the banks of the River Aude. This all appeals to us and we are definitely also in the mood to be a little spoiled.

We are among the first guests on the inviting terrace. There is a wonderful spot in the shade of a beautiful old tree with a protective charisma. The furnishings are completely in style but a little harder than suits my back.

In order to be totally comfortable - we were going to spoil ourselves - I pick up another cushion from one of the other chairs and put it behind me. Straight away a lady comes rushing towards us with an irritated look in her eyes. She starts to tell me off in French. Her eyes seem to send the message that I have committed a deadly sin. I can scarcely understand her, but I can guess it's about the cushion. She mentions something like, *"Autres tourists"* (The other tourists) and I obediently put the cushion back.

Her face has such an accusing look that I'm quite affected by it. My inner child feels wrongly accused and I feel a bit offended.
"Gosh, she's stressed-out," I hear myself saying to Eva.
Later, only a few more tourists join us on the terrace and I could have used another twenty cushions without depriving anyone. While watching the lady, something switches inside me. I see the pain beneath her stress and feel compassion arising and I decide to send her softness. Who knows what her story is?
In the meantime, Eva has changed her beautifully served fish into a battlefield with pins and bones. The gaping mouth with eyes and teeth is still intact and grumpily looks away.

When I look at Eva, we both start laughing because we both think the same thing … What a mess this has become! With a jolly picture of the fish captured in our camera and a big smile on my face I pay the bill. It's time to walk back to our wonderful B&B!
In the evening, I realise that this is already our last night in Alet. It feels like we are being prepared to open ourselves more and more deeply. I feel happy anticipation in my stomach and I can't wait for what the following day will bring.

The Light World is Showing the Way

When we have packed and are back in our car, Eva has the map on her lap. We don't exactly know where to go yet. The only thing we know is that there is a bed for us tonight in Montferrier, close to Montségur. We decide to go back to Lorrie's Angels Gallery; maybe the angels have a message for us. But it turns out to be closed again. I decide to do a meditation in front of the gallery. Eva is restless and goes off for a walk, because it feels to her like we are wasting our time by waiting here. After a while it becomes clear to us that the owner won't be coming. The angels will stay where they are and we won't get a chance to see them.

A few months later I heard that Lorrie was going through an intense process herself and had decided that week to move with her angels. The Languedoc will miss her.

A small route on the map seems to call us, which turns out to be a Cathar route! Our moods are lifting and a Troubadour Castle in Puivert sounds like music to our ears. On the way I see a sign saying Chalabre 10km. Impulsively, I take the exit and it doesn't take long before we see the next exit towards another castle: the Templar Castle of Chalabre.

When we drive into an almost empty car park and I'm about to get out of the car, my eye catches a stone in front of my feet, as I step out. On a reflex I pick it up - I have a thing with stones in special places - and what do I see ... ARC. My heart skips a beat! This is unbelievable. How much more proof do I need that we are on the right track?

It is quiet at the castle. We discover steel rings on the outside of the wall, used to fasten the reins of a horse. They still smell of horses! Once again, we are the only visitors, apart from some children's camps, but they are having a picnic in the forest. The castle has become a kind of educational Templar Castle, where you can do

Found it! The Ark!

all kinds of adventurous knight stuff here. I think they probably did different things here in the old days, but that is - quite rightly - hardly evident.

It is a special experience to be able to go through all the rooms, to look around at liberty, not meeting a single person. We didn't see the particular armour which touched my friend so deeply. When we walk back to the car, after an hour, the Arc-stone burns in my hand, like a trophy found on this sacred quest.

Cheerfully, we continue. Who knows, we might find the church of Roubichoux, that Nicolas mentioned? We weren't able to find it online, but we know it was somewhere between Chalabre and Mirepoix. On the way, we drive through a sweet village and in a flash, I see in between two houses, a beautiful goddess sculpture in the middle of a square. I hit the brakes, turn the car, drive back and park next to the square of the sculpture that had called to me.

It turns out to be a beautiful sculpture ... and ... two maps one of them showing the Eglise of Roubichoux! We find out it's only 6km down the road. I can start to feel it in my lower belly. Wow, this is so well guided. The car easily climbs up the mountain and we arrive in a quiet, hilly and green landscape. There are only a few houses built higher than the road. On the left there is a bare piece of ground where I park the car. We immediately walk towards an old stone arch that seems to be built within the earth. What is this, some kind of shrine? It is covered by a grid with flowers, which really fascinates me, but I can't figure out what it used to be. We walk up the road, towards the few houses.

An old arched wall comes into view and I feel the shivers down my spine. I have been here before. (After this journey, I received more images about the life I lived here, with three children to a great age and I seemed to have something eternal about me.) This felt amazing. It all feels so familiar. Walking around the houses there is no sign of life.

Up on the mound above us we see the church and as I walk around, I try to feel as much as I can. On the hill of the church, which is the highest point of the village, immediately images appear about groups that once came together here to listen to a speaker. What a peaceful atmosphere … The green fields look so inviting! They still carry the energy of the loving wisdom that was spread here.

It makes me speechless and a deep longing comes over me. The Essene woman in me connects to the Holy Family back then. I get so caught up that I almost forget about the stones with the Aramaic inscriptions. However, the church is locked and while Eva stays in

The Eglise (church) in Roubichoux

On our way to the Roubichoux church with the 95-year-old

the cemetery, I walk down to the houses and, in good faith, knock on a door.

There is some noise in the house and an elderly lady in a fresh flowery dress opens the door. Behind her I see a piano. Gosh, that is a very familiar image (in my current life I used to be a concert pianist). In my best French, I tell her that we come from the Pays-Bas, that we heard about their special church and that we would love to visit it. She smiles and says, "How special. I will go and look for the key and I'm sure somebody will come with you."

The key isn't where it is supposed to be, but that's *"Pas de problème"* (No problem). She looks kindly at me and something starts shuffling around behind her. A man appears, a little short of breath and leaning on his stick.

He is also wearing a bright and clean flowery shirt and above that I see a broad smile on a tanned face full of wrinkles. Off we go, up the mountain towards the church with this bright-faced man who tells me on the way, almost out of breath that he has been living there all his life and that he is 95 years old now...

I almost feel guilty that he is climbing up that mountain for us. But he keeps on radiating and smiling and he shows us everything outside the church first. We zigzag across the cemetery, which like

80

the church, is very clean and tidy. He stops to catch his breath every now and then, takes a deep breath and points his stick towards something new about which he'd like to tell us something.

It took them ten years, his sons and volunteers from the area to renovate the church and to make it *"propre"* (clean) again. He pulls something from the outside wall and behind it appears to be the key to the church.

Once inside, my eyes immediately fall on three old stones, big eye-catchers that direct all attention towards them at the entrance. They have clear inscriptions that might be Aramaic!

Even though I don't understand what it says, it touches me deeply. It feels like a greeting and a prayer with which initiates could recognize each other. I inwardly thank the Light World that we have been guided to this place, even though I can't really grasp why we are here and exactly what it is doing for me.

The old man keeps on talking, for more than an hour. He is so full of their beautiful church. He tells us how a cross of dark tiles spontaneously appeared when they tiled the church. It appeared right above where they found an old skeleton, which they discovered under the church.

A part of me has to step away from the idea that I would have liked to meditate in silence in this church. That is not going to happen

Stones from the 1ˢᵗ century with possible Aramaic inscriptions, Roubichoux

this time because more stories need to be told. We also have to look in the tabernacle, which his son built himself, in the wall of the church. Proudly, he shows us all the church's treasures. He starts to win our hearts.

When Eva later says, "Mum, being together with this man actually felt like a deed of love in action!" I realise how our fixed pictures of how something should happen keep us from experiencing something even more beautiful in that moment. When we drive down the mountain later on, we feel deeply touched.

On our way to our next lodging, we refresh ourselves by diving into Lac Montbel. It seems like a blue lagoon to us, right in the middle of the mountains. It is wonderful to cool off in the cold water! We still have bread, cucumber, tomato and avocado in our bags and we enjoy a late afternoon picnic at the edge of the lake. It is the ideal place to contemplate the Essenes and everything they shared, there on the green fields of Roubichoux.

At the end of the afternoon, we arrive at our new destination of Montferrier. A kind woman welcomes us there in an artistic and colourful house. She takes fresh beers out of the fridge for us and disappears again, to allow us to settle in. We plop down on the sofa in the living room, which is part of the guest quarters.

We have the house to ourselves. Again …

Once we have admired all the nice paintings, sculptures and our thick down duvets on the first floor, we ask our hostess whether it is possible to have a nice meal somewhere close. She recommends André, "A lovely man who cooks really well" which sounds great! Within half an hour we are on André's terrace, just outside the village.

We are the only guests; no one else turns up. He slaves away in his kitchen to present us with something very tasty. It goes down really well. However, later on in the night we feel it was a little heavy and we decide to cook for ourselves the next day.

Montségur – The First Leg

During breakfast we both feel we should go and have a look at Montségur. My hiking shoes are ready; I brought them for a reason after all. Here is what I wrote in my diary from that moment on.

01-07 Whooo … The first meeting with Montségur. On the way I was told that we were expected. The road slowly meanders up and suddenly there she is… the mountain that is so familiar. Once we saw her, there was no stopping us; we wanted to get out of the car. There were only about 20 other cars, so it wasn't that busy.
Fortunately, we brought our hiking shoes – the path going up the mountain is very steep, rocky and with lots of little loose stones. But shortly after taking the first few steps alongside the field at the foot of the mountain I already wasn't able to go any further.

Montségur – the first glimpse

We haven't even reached the monument of the Cathars, who walked into the fire because they weren't prepared to renounce their true faith.

It took me too much effort to place one foot in front of the other and I thought 'Did my muscles really got so weak, or are they that tired?' It seemed like I was being held back. However, I continued walking, following Eva who inwardly sensed what was happening. When we reached the monument, I expressed what was happening. At which moment Eva said, "But mum, wasn't that the field where they walked into the fire?" Great, a daughter like that! And back I went, going down, back to the place where I was held back earlier. And then what happened … I completely broke down. I saw images of how the procession of Cathars were coming down the hill, forming one big harmonious entity, I heard a song that was so pure and so full of faith in the Divine…

An overwhelming amount of light is coming down and it is pouring out over me and the field. Tears started to flow because of what I saw inwardly. What a royal radiation they had, those courageous Cathars! They stood in the field opposite Eva and me, and they seemed to be conscious of our presence as well.

Eva starts to remember, Montségur

84

It was incredibly impressive to see them being completely aligned to the Light World, their rock-solid trust and surrender were flowing through me as well in that moment.

Again, I had to weep about the immensity and the memories of 'so that's how it feels when you fully stay true to your higher truth'. We became one with the other dimension, and oh, the spot, the view, and the impressive testimony that they left behind by trusting in a life beyond death, eyes directed towards heaven; 'Into your hands I commend my spirit.'

Out of the blue a lizard appeared on top of the fence on which we had placed our hands. It was slowly walking over Eva's hand and gave me an inquisitive look before I felt sweet, soft little paws going over both of my hands. I literally felt touched by another dimension and realised how they need animals and human beings on Earth to transfer their love.

Walking up again, Eva had a hard time. When we got to the monument for the second time, she was almost fainting. Her solar plexus was blocking up and I inwardly heard some words for her. "You can now let go of all the responsibility you feel for other people." By speaking those words, images came up in her from her former Cathar life. The memories seemed to be releasing from her body. Shaking softly, we walked on hand-in-hand, putting one foot in front of the other, so as to remain very conscious and sensitive. Finally, we reached the little office where you buy tickets to get into the Chateau, but we felt that this was enough for today. We decided not to go on. It was better to continue our path up the next morning.

There are tangible initiation portals on the mountain (most tourists unsuspectingly walk on). For us it felt right to tune into those. We deliberately didn't take any brochures for Montségur, so we could remain as open as possible to what wanted to come through.

Ninety minutes later I wrote as below.

We just experienced a rebirth of Eva. She kept on almost leaving her body and I had to work really hard to keep her grounded, to stay with it. "Mum, please hold my feet," she kept saying. We had to let the energies that wanted to pass through her do their work. There was no connection between the Earthly and divine energies in her solar plexus because of an old belief that those two weren't supposed to come together in a human being.

85

The Divine Feminine, standing on a snake

That belief was still there as an unconscious blockage in her solar plexus and it came up now on account of the memory of her Cathar life. For the Cathars, everything was directed to surrendering to the pure divine; matter was evil, in their view.

This was difficult for Eva who in that lifetime, had carried an enormous Earthly power within her, being a proud and dignified woman.

She had the feeling that she wasn't allowed to live her Earthly power as if it couldn't be joined with the pure divine, which she had also highly developed. Her third eye was completely open, she knew and saw everything and she felt surrounded by a very bright, turquoise, crystal light.

It was clear that these two energies wanted to be connected again within her. She had to lie down on her belly for a long time, feeling the contact with the Earth with the front side of her body. In addition, I had to keep hold of her feet so I could channel the energy in the direction of the Earth. Meanwhile, she couldn't stop shaking, crying and screaming.

An image of a snake queen was coming up; the snake that for many people represents the seduction of the Earthly, of matter, of evil. But in fact, the snake represents the feminine; the Goddess who knows how to carry the divine creative forces in her pelvis.

A little later, the energy of the Dragon flowed through her. It was as if the energies of fire wanted to be spat out so as to put everything in the light. It was truly a process of giving birth to be able to allow everything that wanted to manifest itself through her body without her being conscious of it ...

A radiant, sweaty, fully living young woman is sitting opposite me now. When it was finished and she could lay on her back again and was looking at me, we stretched our left hands out towards each other and we could feel a golden ball of creative power arising between us. This was pure life force! The force, whose secret I feel is being held within the ball of the Ark. The snake-queen amongst us has arisen ...!

Well, it does feel like the true work has begun.

The medieval market square in Mirepoix

Briefly Being Back on Earth

After an extensive shower, lunch and talk we are driving towards Mirepoix. Even though André gave us a wonderful meal last night, it was quite heavy, greasy and a bit too much. We are looking forward to a lighter meal today. So, we get in the car; there's a good chance that there is an organic shop in Mirepoix and they might even sell *pain d'épautre* (spelt bread). Also, Mirepoix is supposed to be a beautiful medieval town that is worth a visit. In the car we are both overthinking all that has happened; it is very quiet. When the sun starts shining on the windows it becomes clear how dirty they are. I try to spray and use the windscreen wipers. Automatically, I make the same move as I'm used to in my own car.

But this car reacts a little differently from what I had expected. I switch the handle again but it only gets worse, the windscreen wipers go mad! Whatever I try, they keep on going. They start to make a weird noise on the dry windows. On this beautiful sunny day, both our back and front windscreen wipers are going up and down, up and down. It starts to work on our smile muscles and soon we have the giggles. With tears in my eyes from laughing, I drive a bit more slowly to be on the safe side. Some French people look pretty astonished when they drive past our car.

From the top down we probably look like a little machine that is frantically trying to clean itself. Eva is cracking herself up laughing. Just before we get to Mirepoix, I manage to get the back windscreen wipers to stop, but the ones on the front window won't stop until I park and turn off the car engine. Gosh, what a day …

When we walk into the picturesque little town, it becomes obvious that so much has happened energetically. Eva in particular has a hard time coping with the Earthly fuss. We walk around the medieval square with lovely little shops and complete a spiritual round in the big cathedral. Again, I see a typical tower that has little beams sticking out of it, which when we get back, I will look up to see whether this has anything to do with the Templars.

Neither of us have space for any new impressions, so we focus on the things we need. The *Lavendula Officinalis* oil is quickly bought; it had already proved its worth in curing blisters and mosquito bites in Montpellier. We also effortlessly discover two organic shops. Such a 'coincidence' that the woman who works in the big shop comes from Brussels, where Eva has been studying for the last two years. During our shopping round it becomes clear how deeply Eva is opening up and how essential it now is to be able to integrate all the changes slowly in peace and quiet.

Soon, we drive back to our B&B with our shopping, including our spelt rye bread. When I turn on the engine, the windscreen wipers resume, wiping frantically back and forth, but now they stop after only one random move. Magical …

It is great to open up the mini laptop and respond to my emails once we are back in the cool silence of our B&B. It is good for us both do something for ourselves for a while. I read an interesting message on the Facebook page of my dear cousin. Her husband is dedicating himself to genealogy, along with being educated in guiding family constellations. A beautiful combination, which confirms that the family trees and bloodlines on paper form some kind of micro-Akashic-records.

My cousin tells us that we have received emails that have to do with my family tree from the Jewish side of the family. This line goes through my mum, via Germany, Poland and Russia, back to France. My great-great-great grandfather was a brave, French warrior who served under Napoleon. He was injured during the invasion in Russia and fell in love with his Russian nurse. This led to the birth of their daughter, the Polish, Helena Maria Isaak, who had already shown herself several times to me. She was the mother of my grandfather Jozef, who died when I was on my way to the Earth – to my mother Helena and my father John. I'm pretty sure I met my grandfather Jozef on the way; I feel a special bond with him.

When I received this genealogical information through the husband of my cousin, I understood why I had been crazy about Poland for some time and that I visited the ancient family ground without knowing it at the time. And why I've been guided towards France this time. Who knows, more information might come up, which will confirm the reason for my current activity in the land of my ancestors.

The clock in the big house rings seven times; time to cook our dinner.

Montségur

The Path of Initiation to the Chateau

After a disturbed night with lots of dreams it gets through to me that we are going to climb to the top of Montségur today. I wonder what we will experience. It feels like Eva has done most of her work yesterday. The connections are made and we are stepping into a field that is already open. A sense of doubt arises briefly when we park at the foot of the mountain on a cloudy morning around 8 o'clock. We are the only visitors and it's very windy. Is that the reason why there's no one else here?

Do they know that we shouldn't climb Montségur with that wind? Maybe we are about to do something that isn't very sensible? I don't know the mountain and don't know what to expect when we go up there. I remember the words of my mother's text-message, "Please be careful in the mountains".

When I look around, I see one other living being: a man, who seems to be lying down very relaxed on a hillside. He seems to represent a comforting presence and I'm sure he has been put there by the Light World to remind me to trust that it is right that we are here now. I feel the urge to go. The 'I' in me is ready and longs to rediscover those energetic portals. This is where initiations and alignments were offered, a means of acknowledging and meeting the divine parts of ourselves and each other.

We take our coats and scarves and walk up the hill towards the monument for the second time. As we are starting our ascent towards the memorial, I feel the goose bumps. This whole journey is one big surrender to our Higher Self. It makes so much sense, to anchor this choice here, on Montségur …

Once we are on our way, it is remarkable how different it feels from the day before! The first openings have been made, I'm not being held back at the field and Eva stays fully in her body when we start the climb. We haven't yet reached the little wooden hut with the ticket booth when we hear someone coming down the mountain. It is a woman, a *bonne femme*; she's probably the wife of the man who is lying down in the grass at the bottom of the hill. After her, we don't meet anyone and all we can hear is the wind blowing in our ears.

When I'm contacting the mountain, I twice feel a clear energy-tornado. Eva experiences too how we become dizzy at certain places and very clear, grounded and activated in others. The first place feels like a guardian-initiation. I see how Cathars took turns here with the guardian job. In their time, there was a lot that needed protection. Their way of life that rose above all, Earthly values and laws were also born out of necessity. Most people didn't have a clue what was really happening on top of that mountain. There was a certain reverence for the *bons hommes et femmes*. They came down the mountain and were pure love and helpfulness.

They healed and shared without asking for anything in return. The *Parfaits*, the highest level of initiates, were more or less enlightened in Earthly eyes. It was quite something, to embody and truly live that ancient knowledge and those mysteries in times when consciousness was so much lower than it is now...

The memorial for the Cathars at the foot of Montségur

The second place that brings me to a halt seems to be a hidden cave. From here, there is a spectacular view over the surroundings. It is completely quiet. The mountain and the valleys surrounding us are permeated with the notion of the great divine, in which we are gradually being taken up. Images arise in me: in that cave initiations and rituals took place and were always carried out by two people. I experience myself as a feminine presence with a channel of light that continues to expand, stretching from the rocks beneath my feet until high above the top of my head. Carefully, a connection is made with my divine masculine half and a wider and more deeply anchored channel arises that takes us to even higher dimensions. A gratefulness flows through my body for the mountain and all those who are present for this awe-inspiring purity and surrender that has been lived here and is still being protected to this day.

The beautiful song *Ubi Caritas et Amor, Deus ibi est (Where there is caring and love, God is present)*, is going through me. We climb on. Words from the reading of Judith Moore arise in me too; *Activate the manna from the Crystal Grail Wombs in the Earth.*
Then the chateau looms up above us. Waves of goose bumps and anticipation are taking turns passing through me making me joyful and stressed at the same time. Up we go, on the solid wooden frame

In the chateau of Montségur

to the entrance. Eva immediately feels pulled towards a spot on the right and nestles herself there and will be meditating for some time. I bend to the left, climb over a few tall rocks and look over the courtyard.

Suddenly, the divine silence that I was experiencing before gives way to intense inner turmoil. My head tells me that I 'have to do' some Light Work here. Since I don't want to interrupt Eva, I keep my distance and make an effort to find the right alignment and the right spot. The turmoil only gets worse. I can't get comfortable and feel disappointed; this wasn't what I had expected on Montségur …

A little later, a smile breaks through on my long face when I hear inwardly: *Hello sweetheart, you don't need to do anything! Just be and*

The gateway opposite the entrance

Enjoying the view at the other side

receive. My ego can't let go straight away. I know this part of myself, the part that always wants 'to make an effort'. But when I consciously let go of any plans, a peace comes over me like a comforting blanket. A family arrives and they walk around, the children climb the rocks and they take photos. After a while, they disappear again through the gate on the other side and are out of sight and earshot. I'm actually starting to enjoy the 'just being'. When the family leaves and we are by ourselves again with the castle and the mountain, Eva and I walk through the other gate.

Something happens here. My crown starts to tingle and is opening. The air that I'm breathing feels fuller with light and oxygen. My lungs are sucking in air and I feel how everything is becoming wider; even my cells want to take a breath. Here, freedom is present! Our view is stunning and the surrounding mountain peaks make us emotional. It is as if there are lots of invisible threads between the mountain peaks; threads of an ancient, divine network that has descended onto Earth. While we connect with it in our own way, we enjoy the divine atmosphere surrounding us, each from our own rock. Such a gift, to be here undisturbed for such a long time in the splendour of the early morning!
After some time, we bless the mountain and all present souls and cautiously start our descent. Lots of rocks are slippery or loose, so

After our Light Work, the sun is shining on the meadow where the pyre burned

we really need to focus. Soon we come across the first tourists who are making their way to the top, chatting loudly. They regard the climbing of Montségur as a tourist or sporty outing. It is after 10 o'clock now, more and more people have to pay an entry fee before they can scramble up the mountain and accomplish their mission.

When we come up to the memorial, we see a spiritual group arriving. I have done group work for about 25 years and I realise how I love to be able to completely follow my own path now. I can tune into why I am somewhere without any fuss, feeling what wants to or may happen. It is about following whatever comes up.

Eva and I are quietly sitting down close to them and we connect with what they are here for. Most of the women have dressed up in their most beautiful garments; red and white gowns are swirling around the memorial. The leader of the group speaks powerful words about how the mountain has been waiting for this moment and for them. Some are crying out loudly over the memorial and I sense a drama in some women who won't make eye contact with us. Others are beaming out a modest love. When a man starts singing, shivers start to run down my spine. I am being touched by the warm sounds and pure soulfulness with which he expresses his message here on the mountain. They perform several rituals and then go up to the castle with flowers, instruments and fully-packed bags to honour the place in their own way.

99

However, we remain outsiders and receive stand-offish looks, as if; 'You are not one of us'. But I don't care. I am very pleased with our morning. We round off our visit to Montségur with a connection to the big light on the meadow where the pyre burned.

I find a special little stone there with an image of a white figure stretching his arms up to the sky against a dark background. How appropriate again! This little brave messenger will go home with us.

When we drive and walk in Montségur village, it feels very sleepy today, above which the castle towers like an anchor. A walk around the valley is signposted as *Le Sentier du Paix*. It's so peaceful and quiet here. As we're getting hungry, we sit down on the outside terrace of a restaurant at the Hotel de Costes. It's midday and we decide to have an extensive meal, so we order as if we have plenty of money.

When I walk indoors to find a toilet, I'm astonished to find a huge cupboard which is filled with spiritual books for sale, including a copy of one of Lars Muhl's books. How is it possible. The sister of my friend had told me about, *The O Manuscript*. A thick book in which Lars describes his own spiritual quest, which mainly takes place on and around Montségur, together with the Seer, a clairvoyant and highly-initiated incarnated Cathar, who helped him remember everything. A book that makes your mouth water, like the French fries that are on our plates right now.

When the waiter comes towards us, I ask him: *"Est-ce que Lars Muhl était souvent là?"* (Does Lars Muhl often come here?) *"Oh, mais oui,"* (Oh yes, very often.) I realise again how I'm walking in the footsteps of many kindred spirits. Four years later, in May 2019, when I am in the Costes restaurant again, this book, *A Journey to Love* is now in their cupboard as well.

Once back in our B&B we want to have a rest. We are both lying on our beds. Suddenly I hear a little shriek coming from behind our shared mini-laptop: "Mum, I've got an email! I'm definitely going to Montpellier from September onwards!"

Together, we look at the email.

Subject : Lettre d'acceptation UM
Date : 02.07.2015 10 :49
Fro : droit-bri, Université Montpellier

Chère étudiante,
Nous sommes heureux de vous transmettre la lettre d'acceptation pour la
faculté de Droit et sciences politiques,
Bien cordialement …

Subject: UM acceptance letter
Date: 07/02/2015 10:49
From: droit-bri, University of Montpellier

Dear student,
We are happy to send you this letter of acceptance for the Faculty of Law
and Political Science,
Best regards …

How beautiful. Our snake queen receives the crown on her work.
Eva can go to the south of France on Erasmus from September. What
divine timing!

Glorious, divine biceps to hold our backs

Sing, Troubadour, About l'Amour

The lizard that walked over my hands at Montségur made me think. What does the lizard stand for? On the internet I found what I was looking for. 'She tells you in each case that you should pay attention to your dreams. She symbolizes the fact that we human beings are more sensitive to subtleties when we learn to be quiet. By becoming quiet we become more receptive to intuitive inspiration. The lizard stands for alertness. She is also a symbol of wellbeing because she can let go of her tail, she shows us the value of being able to let go and to rise again.'

When waking up the next morning, I'm still half in a dream in which there were four men who all wanted a relationship with me. They started to interfere with my life and advised me what to do; annoyingly, they all thought they knew best.

Besides, they didn't have their own lives on track and there were lots of energy leaks about vague and supposedly successful projects, on which they hoped I would give them advice so they could succeed. I turned them all down because I knew it would take too much energy if I connected myself to them. Moreover, I felt that they wouldn't be able to support me at all on the path I wanted to take.

What you dream, you are. There is nothing outside of us. These men showed me my old masculine parts that have been captivated for a long time by Earthly, material successes. I have put enough effort into making a career in this life; it's no longer about that. It's good to realise that my own inner divine muscles really have been released from the stables to serve the way of the Goddess and not the other way around!

That realization feels very powerful. My focus is on this new pathway that I will take, increasingly co-ordinated with my higher parts and with the Light World. Thanks so much, lizard.

After these thoughts, I become conscious of noises coming from the bedroom next door. Our neighbour is walking the Sentier Cathare and it seems like his legs are ready for the next leg of the journey. He takes off while we are having breakfast on the terrace and we see to our great surprise that he is walking on simple plastic flip-flops. Our suitcases have been packed and we hone in on the plans for the day. I'm doubting whether we should stop at the Troubadour Castle in Puivert.

Something within me is saying that I'd like to get to Rennes-le-Château as soon as possible. I have been waiting to visit this place for more than a year! We will drive straight past the castle on the same road, but it feels right to be open to whatever comes up on our path. We have plenty of time and we are being guided anyway.

Once we can see the castle in the distance, an impossible road full of holes and craters zigzagging up the mountain shows itself. It might not be the best idea to drive up with a rental car. We turn into the road and stop to receive advice from other passengers. While I park the car on the side, two motorcyclists come racing down the mountain road. The first one drives on, but the second one stops next to Eva, who is sticking her head out of the window to attract their attention. She tries to make herself heard over the noise of the

The troubadours castle in Puivert

104

Puivert Castle tapestry

roaring motor, but the man shrugs. It was so funny for me to watch! Only after he takes his earplugs out can he hear what she is asking him. He confirms that it is wiser to walk up to the castle. Leaving our car in a safe spot, we perkily walk up in our hiking shoes, glad that we are not modern Cathars wearing plastic flip-flops.

Again, there is a reason for climbing up because the physical exercise awakens powers within us. Once we are within the castle walls and there are quite a bit left of them, we enjoy what we see. There are still so many signs of the true history of Yeshua and Mary Magdalene.

A tapestry shows how (part of) the Holy Family arriving by boat in the south of France, with the Ark included. It is brilliant how the truth has been preserved for us in hidden coding, even within these tapestries! On the next floor we enter the ancient music hall in which the troubadours entertained the noblesse with their songs. There are replicas of instruments from that period and when Eva pushes a button on a music installation, the whole floor is bathed in the ultimate French troubadour atmosphere. They turned courtly love into sounds, as if wrapped in a musical sauce in which they honour the female initiates for their wisdom, purity and sensuality. They sang about her qualities that confer entry to divine worlds. They sang about the Divine Union that we still long to find in every

Captured on the roof of Puivert

relationship. It was all tangible in that powerful and impressive castle, in which only thirteen of the best troubadours in France were allowed to take the noblesse into higher realms.

Once we are on the top of the roof, we enjoy the view and the spontaneous heart connections with the people we meet there. Descending back to Earth, joyfully and fulfilled, a knight is waiting for us (how emblematic). He makes me think about my dream again. Dear heaven, this is a journey packed with precious gifts.

* ♥ *

Off to Rennes-le-Château

We are finally heading to the place where I have energetically been taken to many times at home. I am very excited, like a child who is about to do something very special! Eva asks me, "Mum, are you expecting a lot?" Although I know that it would be good to leave everything open and not to have expectations, I confess.

"Yes, I must admit I am. I'm ready for the abundance of experiences to come. I have been working towards this for a year and I'm ready to be guided. I would love to be confirmed in all that I have seen and felt at home. I hope I will even see the Holy Family themselves."

Maybe these words encouraged the Light World to give clear and understandable signs. We had reached Couiza by that time and I could see the signpost to Rennes-le-Château, which strikes me like

I've been looking forward to this moment for so long ...

Tour Magdala, Rennes-le-Chateau

a heavenly promise.

As we are zigzagging up the mountain, I really get strong vibes and I can't stop talking to Eva, which is why I miss the exit to Les Labadous, the centre where we will be staying for the week.

Oops, too much talking? Or is this part of this magical journey?

Both of us feel that we should continue now towards Rennes-le-Château to sit on a terrace and drink in the atmosphere … to let it sink in that we are really here. In the parking place outside the village, which you have to pay for, it immediately becomes clear that this village has become a tourist attraction after the fame of *The Da Vinci Code*.

I need to catch my breath. Wow, to be here now… I almost can't grasp it! My first gaze is being pulled towards a mountain in the distance and immediately I feel a wave of energy. Th*at must be the Bugarach*, I think, with a feeling of awe. At the same time a little ego voice arises that says, *And what if it's another mountain – you can confer meaning on anything in this way.* Yes, of course, but I also know that I'm careful not to create illusions. A smile comes up; even here the ego-parts of me want to join in, silly ones.

When we walk into the village, I can feel the same energy waves going through me. It is a feeling of welcome and of coming home.

There are some information boards about the tourist hot spots. But we take our own route and make a left into a small street, which is how we get to the outer edge of the village, with the Tour de Magdala in the distance. At the lookout point there is a big panorama image on a panel, showing all the important places in the area. I'm confirmed now that the mountain I noticed is Bugarach.

Beneath the Tour de Magdala there is a little bench. Overwhelmed, we sit down and enjoy the view while we are munching on our last apple. Again, we are almost by ourselves with this breath-taking view over the valley of love, where we can see Les Labadous in the distance.

My eye is caught by a kind of plateau, which lies in between Rennes-le-Château (RLC) and Les Labadous. On the tip of it rises a tower that intrigues us. Totally unexpectedly, the energy of Joseph of Arimathea comes in; and I am wondering whether the plateau has anything to do with him? I can't find anything about it on the

The façade of Villa Bethany, called after the house of Maria Magdalena in Bethany, regularly visited by Yeshua. What a welcome ...

panorama panel, but it will probably soon become clear whether this place is important or not.

Walking on we reach Villa Bethany, the secret house of the former pastor of the village, Abbé Saunière, who – supposedly – discovered the treasures of RLC.

However, we decide not to go into that attractive villa right now, however tempting and inviting it is. We have to visit a bathroom and would love a drink on a terrace. Opposite the villa a familiar sign is spotted – from books I've read – Le Jardin de Marie.

While we are walking towards the toilets, I peer into the garden of the restaurant. Apparently, most Rennies, the inhabitants and regular visitors of RLC, meet here to share the latest news. There is a man sitting at a table and his face looks very familiar to me.

Probably a writer, my head is telling me. Yes, I suppose you can expect such people here. But I'm not here for the VIPs, so after the bathroom visit, we look for a place beneath a large, old chestnut tree and we enjoy our coffee and tea.

We decide to treat ourselves to an apple pie to share, totally against our usual rule of not eating any wheat. It is already almost 2 o'clock and we are really peckish. But I can't help curiously looking across to the man who looks so familiar. I decide to take a walk on the wild side when I'm going to get the bill. A voice within me is saying *Leave him alone, he might indeed be a well-known person and he might simply want to enjoy his coffee quietly.* But when I've finished my coffee and my half of the apple pie, I get up and ignore this critical voice.

On arriving at his table I say: "Excuse me, may I ask you something? Your face seems so familiar to me and I know that if I leave without asking who you are, I will regret that I didn't have the guts to ask you."

The familiar face looks amused, reaches out his hand and responds. "Hi, I'm Tom and this is my wife, Judi."

While I was asking my question the penny had dropped, but I was still thinking; *No, this can't be …?*

Yes, it's definitely true: here sits Tom Kenyon, the global sound healer and the author of, among others, *The Magdalene Manuscript*

David Bailey, Judi Sion, Tom Kenyon and me in the Jardin de Marie

(Alchemy of Horus, Sacred Relationships).

In other words: Tom is a big cheese and an expert in the area of the Hathors, who carry a very high-love vibration from their multidimensional consciousness. He has something multi-dimensional about him as well, I think.

We chat a little and I am introduced to the third person on their table, David Bailey, the pianist who will give a healing piano recital in the church of RLC on Wednesday evening. A little later, I'm telling them about my piano career, the big turn that my life took and how I became completely devoted to spirituality and Christ consciousness. After which Tom says, "I have the feeling that we will meet you again on Wednesday evening. We're going too."

I am vibrating with an inexplicable joy that can't be explained and I say so. Fancy these being the first people I meet in RLC! *What does this mean?* I ask myself, while Eva is taking a picture with their permission. *Should I request a meeting in which we can exchange some things?* My body reacts restlessly. So once again, I decide to surrender to the larger plan.

Flabbergasted, I walk off the terrace. It fascinates me that this is our initiation to our week here at RLC. The Divine Union, in which Yeshua and Mary Magdalene were adepts and the Holy Grail energy. Tom knows how to describe this very well, especially the personal part. He knows what he is talking about. It's like he's supporting my journey energetically, by being there.

I let go of the question *Why* for the moment and we walk on to the church square.

A Church Full of Treasures

How many writers (hundreds?) have examined all the legends, secrets and hidden treasures in and around this church? I can't wait to find out what is waiting for us and align myself to this in silence. It is quiet inside the church. Several people are walking in and out and for a moment a couple is hesitating. In a low voice they're sharing their admiration and recognition of what they see and they

Entering the Rennes-le-Chateau church

try to capture as much as they can with their camera. Eva and I slide in to one of the church benches.

I appear to have seated myself down right next to the sculpture of Mary Magdalene, which radiates a powerful energy. Before me, on the altar, I see an image of the Holy Grail. Beautiful … I'm feeling dizzy. There is so much to see and to feel. I'm being sucked within and I end up in some sort of secret hallway. My attention is being directed to something hidden beneath the church. It is becoming quiet around us; we are the only ones visibly present in the church. And it remains like that, for another hour …

A veil of love is coming down on me. A tear flows down my cheek and I sense this feeling of coming home again. Wow, this is such an intense feeling. Opening up all my antennae, I sense a presence guiding me. I can't help following it, being there with this sacred silence. Before my mind's eye appears a book with a beautiful emanation.

The Book of Love I hear. Is this where it is? Carefully hidden from the ignorant, but 'They who know' have consciously protected it there; trusting that, when humanity is ready, it will be re-discovered and the knowledge can be brought into the world again by initiates.

No treasure hunter who is looking for material treasures will be able to put their hands on it. The book is shrouded in a large, blue haze. It seems to be drifting in front of my chest, carried by invisible hands. My heart, thymus and throat are reacting intensely, like an old cramp that wants to be released.

My chest area becomes very hot and I experience how it starts to open up energetically. Eva starts to cough and I know that we are in a similar alignment again. The love and purity radiated by this book radiates something huge. Nothing within me doubts the presence of Yeshua's own true words in that book beneath this church. It is as if I want to exclaim how powerful this message is: *Be Yourself! Be Truth, be Love!*

Now, a green velvet cloak becomes visible in front of me. I've seen it before when I was meditating in the small house of Mother Mary in Ephesus. Again, this cloak is being put around me and again I feel an immense tenderness and loving presence.

St Marie Madeleine with two stations of the Way of the Cross.

What this week will bring I don't know, but I do know that it's about this, about this soft and at the same time indestructible love that is radiating from Yeshua's book in an almost tangible way.

A golden sun seems to appear on the cover of the book and I feel a connection with the Ark of the Covenant. My chest area starts to soften up. There is truth, harmony and oneness all around, a wave on which I feel carried, with Mary Magdalene next to me.

Full of gratitude I open my eyes and look around carefully. It is swarming with hidden codes, esoteric knowledge, secret messages and revelations about what truly happened with this Holy Family who settled on this - for them so precious - piece of land more than 2,000 years ago. Ancient sanctuaries, Mystery Schools, power-places and healing sources supported them here to maintain the collective field of finely tuned frequencies, so all the connections could remain open. Right now, we are sitting right in the middle of it, which feels divine, surreal and yet very familiar.

When we walk back to the parking spot, we both feel very impressed. How special these days are and how much of a blessing it is to be able to share this together.

A Warm Welcome at Les Labadous

After leaving the parking lot we zigzag down the mountain in slow motion. We're both looking forward to our stay at Les Labadous. What we saw on the website looked very attractive and now we are able to find the road, a little lower down. Again, we were lacking eyes and ears to be able to perceive all the beauty as we are entering the valley. Once at Les Labadous, we are greeted with a strange howl from the bushes.

I am smiling inwardly, thinking about the song of a famous Dutch comedian Toon Herman's *What is hustling there in the bushes?* but to be sure we keep our distance.

Our apartment at Les Labadous

The noise was made by Roua; an old, stray dog who appeared at Les Labadous one day and never left. What a clever animal. We walk through the gate and look around with open mouths. Wow, such a beautiful and spacious property! A gentle and modest man comes to welcome us, Axel. He is a loyal servant, handyman and a Guardian Angel, we soon discover. With the patience of a saint, he shows us around the premises. In passing he tells us that Tom Kenyon and Judi Sion are staying "over there" (he points at a large building opposite our apartment); they are co-owners of Les Labadous.

Holy Cow... I think, well, if we are meant to exchange something energetically, the Light World has made it easy for me. It is all allowed to unfold effortlessly and without interference from the personality. That is how it works, in the fifth dimension, right?

Axel opens the door of our apartment. Wow, it's huge, very spacious and light. From our terrace we look over the beautiful garden in which hammocks are waiting for us. We settle into our new place and take our time to discover and get to know everything. During the afternoon, more and more guests of Les Labadous appear. In this magical happening it seems to speak for itself that they turn out to be the beautifully dressed up group that we saw at Montségur earlier today. Three of them were married in this sacred land. Now, can you blame them? Here, in this garden, connections emerge between us and they openly start to share their experiences.

Our next-door neighbours are a whispering Spanish couple; we already saw them in the church with their camera. It's ideal to have these quiet people as our neighbours.

After a rest we get back into the car because our fridge needs to be filled up. Thanks to Axel's detailed help and directions we now know where to find the shops. After that we head back up the hill again to get ourselves a meal in the well-shaded garden of the pastor's house-keeper, le Jardin de Marie. We continue to detach from the poverty consciousness!

In the evening we meet Joke, who has been the owner of Les Labadous together with her ex-husband Jaap for more than 15 years, and her current partner Franklin. They live in the large house and work day and night to make each guest's stay as pleasant and complete as possible. Joke has been doing this for 15 years now and is ready for a new owner to take over – someone who would like to continue in the same atmosphere. Les Labadous has now been for sale for five years.

At the end of each day Joke and Franklin make a round of the property, in the course of which they greet everyone who is open. Full of warm engagement they enquire about the experiences and discoveries of the day. It's as if we're taken into a family who comes and goes, but is connected forever. This place feels very rich, incredibly healing, valuable, charming and still fully encompassed by the beneficial legacy of all who served the Christ consciousness. No wonder that it feels like home for many spiritual groups coming from all across the world.

How Sir Galahad, Sir Bors and Sir Percival were fed with the San Grael.
Painting by Dante Gabriel Rossetti

San Greal and Sang Real

After a restless night, in which I was kept awake by the intense energy of the wedding group, we both get up with the feeling that we should take it easy today. When I'm picking a huge artichoke for our dinner from the vegetable garden, I see RLC bathing in the sunlight in the distance. The golden glow that surrounds this place on Earth is breathtaking …

Here, in the safe and nourishing valleys surrounding RLC up to a distance of about 20kms, lots of traces, signs, treasures and secrets have been found. There is a reason why this area is very popular with seekers, spiritual and material ones. Hundreds of books have been written about the caves, grounds and hidden places being full of priceless ancient heritage, which are literally worth their weight in gold. They might even contain Templar treasures from Jerusalem, brought to the south of France just before the city was besieged. Many people believe that among them are the real, or replicas of the Ark of the Covenant and the Holy Grail. People who still think that it is about a material treasure are in this case looking for the San Greal (Holy Grail).

But there is an energetic treasure! The mountain, sources, churches and sanctuaries in the surroundings are situated in sacred geometrical shapes the same distance from each other, all of which is visible when they are aligned and connected on a map. They form an exact copy of the sacred land of Israel. This isn't a coincidence! For instance, the Moses Mountain in the Sinaï and the Temple Mount close to Jerusalem are energetically similar to Pic de Bugarach and Pech Cardou, which are just a stones' throw away from where we are now. If you look closely, you can see hidden signs of a Messianic bloodline everywhere: Sang Real, the royal blood.

In the church of RLC there are two very special sculptures of Mary and Joseph hanging on the wall on both sides of the altar, like silent witnesses. Both are holding a child. Are they two of Jesus' children?

121

Or is this about one Jesus who died on the cross, according to the Vatican and another who lived in the Languedoc after a recovery period among healing sources? The descendants of Anna, Mother Mary, Josef of Arimathea, Yeshua and Mary Magdalene have been able to live their mission here, undisturbed and protected. Until the Romans extended their trade routes to the south of France and began to see these Essene communities as a threat. People have attempted to destroy or possess every small trace of proof of the legacy from these pure bloodlines and the true Christ consciousness that was based on love. They wanted to eradicate them, or at least get them under control with their own religion based on fear and power.

Lots of the history here is hidden in the earth, the mountains, the stones, sources, sculptures, paintings, tapestries, songs and stories that have guarded the truth in secret.

Three hours later we've had breakfast and we can hang out our laundry that Axel had washed for us. It's hot and quite humid, the sun is high in the sky and I might just as well hang myself out to dry too. On the veranda of the big house there is an internet connection and it takes us some time to catch up with all the messages from the home front; there is so much to share. We also need a bit of space for ourselves to be able to integrate everything so we take some quiet time. I don't expect we'll be doing much more today than going back to the village to visit the mysterious house of Abbé Saunière.

Halfway through the afternoon we're taking a leisurely drive to the village. Villa Bethany is meant to reveal a lot to 'those who have the eyes to see' and with appropriate curiosity we buy an entry ticket. There are rumours that this villa was built on the remains of a house in which Mary Magdalene resided for some time.

The pastor, Bérenger Saunière had apparently 'by chance' discovered ancient documents in one of the pillars during a renovation of the altar in the church. Until today nobody really knows what was written on those documents. But it soon became clear that it concerned immensely valuable secrets.

Both the church and the villa were completely renovated in no time and in unheard of luxurious fashion for a poor village pastor. It's been said that either the Vatican or rich nobility had given him hush money. Hidden chambers were opened, a lot was happening

Villa Bethany, Saunière's room

in the basements under the buildings, in caves and underground passageways, which had probably been there for centuries. Something was hidden here that wasn't to fall into the hands of the world and especially not the Vatican. Saunière died with all his secrets sealed on his lips and a few years later his house-keeper Marie Dénarnaud followed him silently. The only thing they ever said was that 'The people in RLC were walking on gold without knowing it'. In addition, mysterious codes have been left on paintings, tombs and sculptures and many people have tried to decipher these in vain and to many treasure hunter's great frustration.

In the villa, there is much to see and to be speculated about. There is a magical museum, but today that is too much for us. It is very hot both inside and outside and we are tired. It doesn't take us long to leave the village. In the village bookshop we buy a detailed map of the surroundings, a few packets of divine incense and we drive back to our hammocks and silence.

In the evening Roua, the old dog suddenly starts howling heart-wrenchingly. I wonder what is going on and it soon becomes clear. His owner has arrived!

123

Jaap Rameijer, former owner
of Les Labadous and writer
of beautiful, inspiring books

Soon we're shaking hands with Jaap Rameijer and a friend who are staying in the apartment next to us. We have a chat and in the meantime I'm very curious whether we can take a tour together with Jaap – he knows everything about these surroundings. I loved Part 3 of his books, *The Secret Messages of Rennes-le-Château*. I'm looking forward to buying Parts 1 and 2 from him too, for which I left extra space in my suitcase.

Bugarach

We get up fresh and perky the next morning. We'll be doing Light Work today! But … there is so much to 'do', it's hard to make the right choice out of all these beautiful places. I've been dreaming of going to the Fontaine des Amours for some years now. This magical place consists of sacred sources in the middle of a fairy forest. For more than 2000 years, many rituals and baptisms took place in these natural water basins, in complete alignment with the Light World. Once, in a regression, I saw Joseph of Arimathea giving Grail initiations here.

When this was confirmed some time ago, this evoked a lot of old pain and homesickness within me. I knew that this had been a life for me in which I was completely happy, completely aligned with

A gateway towards higher dimensions. The top of the Bugarach is older than its bottom. On 21/12/2012 hundreds of people gathered here for the expected Apocalypse.

the Source and almost completely uninterrupted by any shadow side of my personality. A part of me can't wait to go to the Fontaine des Amours, but another part of me wants to postpone it a little bit.

With the new map and, of course, a water bottle within reach we take off. I trust that wherever the car wants to bring us is the right way. There are lots of small roads here, only known by the locals, but with this detailed map we'll probably find our way. Axel showed me a beautiful route on the map and he's right; the road is stunning. It's part of the Sentier Cathare. On the way we should come across an exit towards Fontaine des Amours. But before we can take it, we have already passed it. We think about turning around, but the road is quite narrow and oddly enough there are a lot of cars coming the other way so we can't do that.

It was already clear to us that there is not so much oncoming traffic on the winding mountain roads; we feel protected when we are driving around. However, this time the oncoming cars prevent us from turning around. We need some time to switch, but it seems meant to be that we are going to Bugarach! From the couch in my home in Zutphen this mountain had already seemed very impressive to me. This turns out to be the same in 3D! We drive around this masculine and magical mountain for about 20 minutes before we find a suitable place to park. From now on we let our feelings guide us to what wants to happen.

At 11h22 we put the first foot on the mountain. Again, the sun is burning down on us, so we decide to walk on until we find a beautiful meditation space in the shade.

The earth is black, red and bone-dry beneath our feet. There is no shade yet in sight. We continue to walk on in a brisk pace - it feels like a masculine walk. Something within us tells us to enjoy this process consciously - isn't it special to walk on holy ground which is thought to have housed an Essene Mystery School? And that within the mountain a secret landing place for UFOs might be situated? In any case, it is the place to open up our multidimensional consciousness!

The energy is very high. It takes us a lot of effort to walk here. We reach an area that harbours a bit more shade and the pastures give some air to the walk. After this part, a more humid and woodland part presents itself, where electrified barbed wire is taut along the narrow path. We have to watch out not to touch it. However subtle it is, it feels like a counter force. As a marker point, there is a provocative looking forest spirit in a big tree root. We're sure we'll soon find a place with a beautiful view on the impressive peak. After an extra leg through the many bushes, it seems that the mosquitos have found us and our moods descend to a lower consciousness. We both get into a struggle with ourselves while in the meantime we can't do anything else than continue because it doesn't feel right to turn around and head back.

I keep hearing myself say, *Just a little further and then we will sit down somewhere, okay?* But this little further seems to continue forever. The tension rises even further. Out of the blue, I start a conversation with the mountain. "What do you want to give me? And what is it that you need from me?" I ask.

An answer comes. *I want to give you security and trust,* I ask my heart what it would like to give to the mountain it immediately responds

Can you see the Patriarch/Sphinx in the Bugarach?

127

with *gratitude*. Funnily enough, I feel anything but gratitude in this moment. I'm tense and I'm wondering whether we are doing the right thing. But then we arrive in another area which is very spacious and has huge white rocks. On one of them a huge heart has been formed out of green moss. There is a purity here that touches my heart and the tension is lessening somewhat. Along the way, I find a flat stone in the shape of a big heart and while I'm holding it, I can feel its power. Suddenly the vegetation ceases to exist and we are above the tree line. The view is amazing on both sides. The point where we are would be a beautiful spot to sit down if it hadn't been for the very steep slopes on both sides of the path, both up and down.

However, neither of us feels like going on, so I move a little higher up on the path to make space for Eva. Eva is always very trusting, but she now asks me while turning around towards me, "Mum, are you sure you're alright there? You could easily slide down!" and I break into a sweat.

I'm sitting on a spot where I normally would never place myself, being afraid of heights. I look up, thinking about possible alien spectators and become conscious of myself being completely tensed up. Nonetheless, I'm a hundred percent sure that this is the place to be right now. So, I decide to be present with my completely tensed up body. I start to communicate inwardly with the mountain again. I confess that I'm about to freeze with fear, which might have to do with a former life in which I fell off a mountain. Two months later this is confirmed, when I am inwardly being taken to Mount Fuji in Japan, a sacred mountain too off which I fell, or rather, I was pushed.

My solar plexus, belly and base chakra are all cramped up. I feel very closed off and my breath is high in my chest. When I share this with Eva, she tells me she's also inwardly dealing with her fears. We decide to acknowledge all that there is and share it with the mountain. I direct my attention inwards, to my grounding. I want to become one with the mountain and the only way to do that is to be present here. So, I visualize a rock of trust in my pelvic area.

The mountain is one big chunk of trust and a fatherly comfort comes over me. While I sink even more deeply into the mountain,

I feel welcomed and safe. The tension decreases so much that my heart feels touched. When I look up towards the high bare solid rocks, it's like we're in the lap of the Patriarch who is enfolding and protecting us.

From this quiet space I can feel that I'm thirsty and I take a sip of water from my bottle. My mobile phone shows it is 13.13 o'clock. Feeling more relaxed, I take some pictures. Behind me on the ground I see

Pic de Bugarach, Mountain of God

a special stone that reminds me of Moses, who received the Tablets of the Testimony on his mountain in the Sinai. This mountain is an energetic copy of that one and with this realisation in mind, I pick up the stone.

On my back I can feel an Old Wise One rising and almost simultaneously Eva and I start making sounds. They spontaneously rise up within us and we offer them to the mountain and the valley. The waves that are flowing through us become louder and louder and I feel myself opening up more and more. The energy starts to spin and a feeling of oneness starts to arise in every fibre of my being. We vibrate with the mountain and the mountain vibrates with us. Wow, so much power! Whereas I felt like a vulnerable lamb before, now the primal power of a lioness comes through me. Like two warriors, we give our primal screams to the world. I can understand now why this mountain is called the Mountain of God. It invites you to come into your full power with all that you are.

Still feeling 'on fire', as we walk back to the car, we realise how the hike on this mountain aligns with a journey through the chakras. It speaks for itself that the crown chakra is opened at the top of the mountain. And from the throat chakra, where we sounded, we were being invited to share our truth with the world.

There is the white rock with the green heart (heart chakra) and beneath it the forest spirit that provocatively looks into my solar plexus. Under that are the more enjoyable pastures with wild flowers (sacral chakra) and at the foot of the mountain, the Earthly life in the burning sun on the dark earth (base chakra). Full of amazement about all of this, we walk down. When we get back into the car, we realise only too well that we've been outside time and in another dimension.

Our empty bellies guide us to the only restaurant open in the village. In the back there is an improvised garden terrace with a view of the mountain. Under the parasol we enjoy our big plate of salad while the owner makes us laugh, he seems slightly eccentric. Eva says, "It looks like he can't cope with the high energy here". She turns out to be exactly right because later, I hear that many foreigners who bought a house in this village out of enthusiasm for the magical

Eglise (church) de Bugarach

energy here, had to sell a few months later because they couldn't stand the high frequencies and became ill.

The jolly owner asks what we are planning to do in the afternoon and I tell him that we would like to go and see the church. *"Mais non!"* he exclaims. "A woman like you doesn't belong in a church! There's nothing for you there, right? What are you going to do there?"
Well, that's not so easy to explain... So, I smile and we both resolutely walk off towards the church. We push open the heavy wooden entry gate and there is nobody to be seen.
A little later, we stride down the aisle towards the altar. It looks and feels like a Divine Union Temple, where you naturally align with your divine love energy. In the large blue overarching firmaments hundreds of golden stars are shining. In disguised sculptures we discover countless signs that Yeshua and Mary Magdalene indeed were married and had children. In several places in the church, we see the letters S&R painted in elegant curled writing and we wonder what they mean because we have come across these letters in almost every church in this region.

From the connection between my heart and crown, a blue light arises, which merges with the light in the church. When I sit down at the foot of the altar, my body feels very soft, tender and transparent. This is very different from when we started our mountain walk this morning. Later this makes total sense; I discover that this church is right on the ley line that merges the masculine and feminine Christ energy! When I connect this energy with the masculine mountain within myself, the work for today feels done. We long for a quiet place to integrate these new 'downloads'.

Wouldn't be it total bliss to close this day with visiting the Fontaine des Amours? my mind says. We are tired, but we practically pass right by it and who doesn't want to take a bath in a fountain of love? We can see the road-signs leading to it. However, we seem to have

The sign of La Fontaine des Amours, The Fountain of the Beloveds

passed it because there are no more parked cars along the road and we don't see any more signs. "I think you have to turn around mum," Eva says. This isn't easy, I need to drive on for quite some time before I find a suitable place to turn the car. Eventually, we see the wooden pedestrian sign with the arrow pointing down and I manage to park the car next to a cliff under which, in the valley the loving water is flowing.

Immediately disappointment comes up. It is very busy, with lots of people screaming, splashing and diving into the basin. Young people are competing for the most beautiful dive of the day with lots of noise. It doesn't look like the peaceful place that I had sensed in my meditations back home at all. We decide to slip through all the bathing suits, towels and coolboxes to get to the water and put our toes in anyway. *Mmm that feels great.* Despite everything, the energy of the place is working on my lower chakras, seeing me laying here with a loved one in quieter times.

When I connect to the fairy forest surrounding us, I understand that the timing isn't right now. I will come back at a quieter and better moment, to honour the place and to connect with its serenity and beauty and the flowing source of love that she is and what she's meant for.

To Serres at the foot of Pech Cardou, with the ruins of the Castle de Blanchefort

Comme Une/As One by Luke Owen

On our way back towards les Labadous, I catch a glimpse of the ruin of Chateau de Blanchefort, high up on a mountain top. It is positioned straight across from Pech Cardou, which is also on our list to visit in the coming days.

Within this holy, feminine mountain you will find a copy of the divine geometry of the Temple of Solomon in which initiations took place and apparently still do. Was this where the Ark of the Covenant or other treasures were hidden? I suspect that a part of the original content can still be present there. I feel 12 subterranean hallways connected with this Temple. Only the highest of initiates knew about those. From the Chateau de Blanchefort there was continuous surveillance and protection of what was hidden here, among others by the Templars. It wouldn't surprise me if this was the place described in the Grail novel *Floris and the Blancefloer*, which touched me so deeply when I was in high school and I wrote a paper about it.

The Hautpoul family were the owners of Chateau de Blanchefort. They were pure descendants of the bloodline of Yeshua and Mary Magdalene and the last aristocratic family who held the family tree - or a copy of it - in their possession. By showing me this it feels like my guides had already connected me with our next project. After realising this, the work really feels done for today.

That evening I sit on the veranda in front of the big house, editing my notes and sending WhatsApp messages. I notice there is a man who I hadn't seen before. We greet each other and I look into very gentle eyes. His voice is quiet, his whole being radiates humility. He looks a little like a lost Essene behind a laptop. His long hair gives me a comfortable familiar feeling. It is nice to sit there together and round off the day in the silence of a beautiful evening beneath the starry sky.

Luke Owen at his gallery in Rennes-le-Chateau

Unexpectedly Being Born Again

A searing headache wakes me up the next morning. It feels like my skull is bursting open from my third eye. I look at the alarm clock and see 6.22am. Lucky me, I can sleep for another few hours. Fortunately, a few hours later the headache is a lot less intense. Relieved, I walk to the big house to get milk for my coffee.

There is the Essene again. His charisma is kind of saying 'take it easy' and this seems like a wonderful affirmation for the day. A lot that happened yesterday needs to be digested today. While I'm preparing for a day to stay at home, Eva comes running towards me. "Mum, if we like, we can come with Jaap and two friends to the cave of Mary Magdalene and the Source of the Mother Goddess! But we'd have to pack our stuff straight away because we'll leave soon; they only have a few hours spare time."

Wow ... what an opportunity! I had been thinking about the caves a lot, and had been told that it is hard to find them if you don't know the place. For a moment I wonder whether this is truly the right thing to do now, but before I grant myself the time to let the answer come, one foot is already in my walking shoes. A little later, together with his friend Door, we sit in Jaap's big white four-wheel drive, waiting for Jaap himself. After a few minutes he appears, together with the Essene.

My jaws drop when he gets into the car and sits next to me and introduces himself.

"Hi, I am Luke Owen."

My gosh, is this the Luke Owen, the RLC artist!

One of my Facebook friends was Val Wineyard, who has written several books about the Holy Family and their secret life here. On her page I once read, *Luke is back in town!* After which, she told us that he had to go to the UK because of painful family circumstances, but that he was back in RLC now to heal himself and any passers-by with his soulful creations. This humble Essene turns out to be the painter who opened a gallery at probably the most beautiful spot in RLC. He translates the most beautiful messages of love and light into colours that go straight into your heart.

When the five of us are heading towards RLC, I realise that we are being given another gift today. Luke tells us a little bit about his life and that he sometimes spends time at Les Labadous. He asks about me and Eva with genuine interest.

After the short introduction, we have already reached the other end of the village. Eva and I promise him that we will visit him in his gallery in the coming days and Luke gets out of the car, thanking Jaap for the ride.

Our eyes and ears are now directed towards the front of the car. Jaap starts to tell us extensively about the places that we pass and that we will visit. This trip is mainly on request of his dear friend Door, who comes here to recharge. She was eager to visit the caves today before she heads home again.

We first drive to the Source of the Mother Goddess. This is clearly visible. The healing, ferrous spring water has coloured the edge brown-red, which makes it even more like a feminine stream. On both sides of the double water flow there is an entrance towards a

The Source of the Mother Goddess

138

low cave, which is very special. They're like two ovaries that give access to the sacred space behind it.

We connect with the moist soil - it feels like a place to be in the wellness of the silence to allow and honour the earth power of the Mother within ourselves. However, we don't have so much time now, so after a sip of the source we go on to the next place.

Jaap tells us we can reach this place with our rental car as well, but we haven't paid clear attention. It seems to speak for itself, the way to the source and we decide inwardly to come back here later. Funnily enough, we tried to come back here twice but we never found it again; apparently this has to wait until the next journey.

We drive past a local farmer where we can buy local wine. Delicious wine, we find out later. With the goodies in the back, we enter a wilder landscape. Jaap's sturdy car has no problem with that and soon we arrive at the path to the Mary Magdalene caves. With our bags and water, we closely follow Jaap. At first, the path goes fairly straight through a dry grassy landscape. Both Jaap and Door are carrying walking sticks and he tells us that those are important here, because of the snakes that will get out of the way when they hear the ticking of the sticks. Jaap also says that in one of the books about Mary Magdalene it is written how someone died of a snake bite in this valley!

The path starts to twist and turn and Jaap tells us, "*Watch out, it may be slippery here, every now and then.*" He sometimes stops to hold out his stick to give us a grip on the steep descent. I now understand why there are about 30 sticks lying around at les Labadous and why everyone always takes a stick when they go somewhere! They come in very handy, are multi-functional and are definitely not the Nordic walking hype sticks. I feel grateful that we are not by ourselves here; I wouldn't have wanted to take this tour without guidance. The last bit of the path is along a narrow ledge with a steep cliff. It strikes us that this part of the path is completely white. After some more acrobatic manoeuvres we stand in front of two caves, to the left the Mary Magdalene cave, and to the right the cave of Birth. We go into the left cave first. Wow, it carries a very soft energy. The cave feels very tender and in return my feelings for this place are very loving. But, I don't recognise the cave, shape-wise.

139

Eva in the Mary Magdalene cave

When Jaap tells us that the original cave was much deeper and lower on the inside, but that because of rainfall more and more earth has accumulated on the bottom, I get goose bumps. Now I understand why the original image that I received from the cave at home didn't match with what I see now.

I close my eyes and receive images of another time. It is like there are veils sliding over me. My heart is overflowing with love for all the women, priestesses and goddesses who have ever been in this cave. I experience more and more women in the cave. Together with them I'm dressed in a creamy-coloured gown. Eva and I both feel a soul sister-connection with each woman. Every woman who lets her feelings and tears flow here contributes to the large collective field of surrender, truth and goddess-truth. It is a big warm cloak of love that is surrounding us here and it is a pity that we can't stay longer. There is also time however to visit the Birthing Cave. We climb up through the mini-birth canal. When we are inside, I connect to my own descent into this life, my own time in the uterus. Wow, that is a whole different energy. The Earthly field I got into is one of shame and guilt. I have been born with a false and inherited feeling of guilt of *I'm sorry to be here.* I feel that old pain coming up immediately.

Next to me I can hear Eva breathing with difficulty; her coming into this Earthly life wasn't rosy either. Both she and I balanced on a dodgy edge at her birth after a long evening and night full of contractions. I lost two and a half litres of blood and I heard later that it was very worrying. Her difficult start in this life took both of us a long time to process.

Even though we are in a hurry; I decide that I want to go for truth now and I ask Jaap and Door if they want to welcome me onto Earth once more. I invite them to tell me, "How wonderful that you're here. We love you!" They lovingly empathise with their role and when I come out of the cave, I dive into four loving arms that intimately embrace me and show me how much they are there for me.

After a few tears, my sadness quickly changes into sincere joy. Right

Born again

141

*The Cave of Birth after our
visit (with orbs)*

there, I realise that the old mistake of wanting to go away again, away from duality and back home, is fully seen through and is replaced by, *This is where I want to be. This is my place.*

I turn around to witness my daughter who very consciously would like to be birthed again. Jaap asks, "And Eva, what is your story?" Eva shares, her tears start to flow and I can feel the old pain coming up again too. It was completely in the hands of God whether we would both make it back to Earth during Eva's birth.

What an incredible gift it is for her, to be born again here. I feel her and see how she is being received by the same four loving arms. But instead of seeing a little girl who only just made it, I see a powerful woman who will live her mission on Earth very decisively, no matter what. I thank the heavens for this incredibly beautiful moment. And hereby I'd like to thank Jaap and Door again for making this possible - it was of eternal value.

Portal Day at Pech Cardou (07/07)

While we celebrate our rebirth and stuff our breakfast table with all sorts of delicacies, my attention is being drawn to the field in front of us. The women's group who has been here now for a couple of days is going through different layers of emotions and is getting ready to start moving to music from the portable CD player.

The by now familiar synthesizer music reaches my ears and I ask Eva: "Are you having the same experience? The first day that I heard this electronic noise I thought 'Oh no, will we hear this every day at breakfast now?' But I actually started to like it. I will miss it when it's not there anymore."

Eva knows exactly what I'm talking about and from our little terrace we sway along with the rhythm that becomes slower and slower. After a few days all the external appearances disappear and completely different women appear. Like-minded people, as vulnerable, powerful, wounded and searching as any other human being who is walking around in duality. We are all looking for the love with which we can finally embrace ourselves.

What would it have been like for Mary Magdalene to have walked around here? It must have been quite something to be such a wise, highly-initiated woman in her time. Her task, to take her position next to her beloved Rabbouni ... She somehow knew what was about to happen; it must have been almost impossible to bear that all. But she also must have known how their incredible gift would change humanity on Earth for good! What a task ...!

This was only possible because of their ultimate surrender to the Divine Plan, in which our human part bows it head and surrenders to; 'Thy will be done'.

Only then can the universal and divine forces work through a human being and great things can happen.

A lonely Mary Magdalene
in the cave of Monastere de
Carol in Baulou
(credit Jaap Rameijer)

Well, here I am, in the surroundings where this all happened, in total surrender to what is the right thing in the Divine Plan. To what extent can we align to what wants to happen today? We react in an extreme fashion to all places here. How special is it that we also sometimes seemingly experience very little from the higher dimensions. However, we often notice afterwards that the intended gift has been implemented on other levels anyway. Today, our bodies ask for feminine softness and tenderness. How suitable it is to connect with a feminine sacred mountain.

Pech Cardou, with the Temple of Solomon there, is hidden deep within the earth. All its secrets are connected with divine creative forces and with the descendants of Yeshua and Mary Magdalene. I can feel that this portal day carries something special, like a silent expectation when I direct my attention inwardly.

Soon we are in the car driving towards Pech Cardou; as always Eva is guiding me with the map in her hands. We wait for an impulse from inside. Suddenly we both whisper, almost simultaneously; "Whooooooooow!"

"Do you see that villa on the left there? It's got something! It seems so familiar," I say.

"Yes," Eva replies. "I think so too! I'm getting a *déjà-vu*-feeling as well!"

As if hypnotized, I park the car on the roadside and we extend our feeling antennae over the tarmac to the other side of the road. I immediately tune into a session that I did a few months ago. Would this be ...? *Yes, it definitely is,* a voice within me says. I give Eva a brief version of this session.

The occasion for this was that I had been carrying around a huge anger for some time, which was triggered especially by men with a certain character trait. They could unleash a rage in me, with a need to kick and scold, so it seemed interesting to find out what was actually beneath it all. While feeling into it, I entered into a former life in France, where I was a lady of noble birth who owned several big villas which I wanted to renovate to turn into spiritual centres for children. I was a real powerhouse, a wise and free woman who

Chateau de Serres across from Pech Cardou

145

wasn't scared of anything. However, my husband at the time was a wimp, he couldn't cope with me and he unexpectedly left me. Because of this I lost some of my possessions and I couldn't manifest my beautiful plan that was truly based on pure and idealistic ideas. I can still see the notables sitting there with their rigid pomposity, with an arrogant *air d'importance* when they told me what I would lose. The French Ladyship within me had wanted to kill them!

Anyway, here we are with our little car, going to do something at Pech Cardou but we both feel called by this place. So, I turn onto a parking place directed towards the valley at the Pech Cardou, diagonally opposite the villa, which looks like a little castle.

Our jaws drop again and Eva is getting overexcited. Like an enlightened young girl, she jumps out of the car, towards the green field with herbal garden.

"Mum, I really want to spend some time walking around here!" she stresses.

A clear stream runs through the valley. It reminds me to go with the flow and to follow what touches us. And this touches us, that's for sure. Eva is enchanted and seems to be able to light up the whole world with her radiant face.

"This is where I lived," she says, "this was the happy life that showed up in the reading with Judith!" Yes, she is right, I can feel it too. We

Eva in the garden in Serres

146

Serres, view from the church towards Pech Cardou

both walk around with our personal memories and I experience that many timelines are coming together.

While our chakras are opening up effortlessly through all the lovingness that we experience around us, we take pictures of this valley, filled with light that seems to contain a lot of *Manna*. We admire the carefully tended herbal garden in the green valley and when we say that the love with which this garden is kept is very tangible, a man appears with a wheelbarrow. He greets us like dear friends and disappears again through the herbal garden, between the trees at the foot of the mountain, leaving us behind with a surprising feeling of being known. Like we are picking up where we left off.

Wondering what else will be revealed, we walk across a beautifully renovated Roman arched bridge, that takes us further into the village of Serres. At 11 o'clock we walk into the quiet church, straight across from Pech Cardou. It's like I'm entering a big uterus, being taken into the same soft enveloping cloak as in Mary Magdalene's cave. The salmon-pink, sandy atmosphere here is breathing pure love.

A wave of emotion shoots through me when I become conscious of what is painted on the ceiling a little further on. There is not

147

one cross, but two, with both the pedestals and arms connected. Is this about Yeshua and Mary Magdalene, the divine masculine and feminine? Everything comes together here in the arms of those two Beloveds. There are two murals on both sides of the altar. One seems to show a female figure, but she's almost invisible. I realise how painfully true this is in time. Mary Magdalene, condemned and rendered as invisible as possible by the church. On the other wall, I can clearly see Yeshua, who holds a sphere (globe) in his hands. It is true that he held the fate of planet Earth in his hands during his incarnation. His descent to Earth was carefully prepared in the higher spheres and by the initiates on Earth that who knew about it. He embodied the highest divine love as a human being, so his spiritual power and pure DNA could come to Earth, by means of which the way towards higher love and consciousness was opened for everybody. The two crosses are standing there as silent witnesses of the fact that love and truth can conquer all.

We drink in this beneficial energy and give our gratitude to every corner of this healing church. I feel encouraged to go on with this

Interior of the church with the two crosses! To the right you can see a bust of Jeanne d'Arc

holy quest. There is still so much confusion in the unconscious layers of human beings, a lot of cloudiness and manipulation by the ego. I experience it as a part of my task to keep this completely pure and conscious. The so-called holy love and paths to God have become a personal possession and a way to manipulation; it is time to bring this to the light and to heal it.

From the church I'm being pulled towards the little castle. But Eva needs to go to the bathroom and we see a sign saying Theatre, which we follow. This is a pretty random action because the village is deserted and it doesn't look like there will be an open door to a theatre with a bathroom in it. While we are already walking out of the village without having seen a theatre, it becomes clear that the bathroom stop should take place behind some bushes.

Walking back to the car, two statues of squirrels gaze on us. My favourite animals!

For Eva a memory of a childhood book comes up - she can't remember the title. But it feels like it's important and when it pops up in her head later that day, it makes perfect sense. The title was, *Maybe They Knew Everything*. It is a collection of short stories by Toon Tellegen in which the animals are being described in all their beauty, uniqueness and truth in an endearing way. How fitting that this wants to be remembered on this spot.

Here, truth is lurking at Pech Cardou and whatever there is under or in this mountain, it is important. It is guarded for a reason. Some ancient sacred knowledge is hidden here, being embodied by those who served the ultimate and gave their lives for it. I get a similar feeling when we walk around the castle. At the driveway is a sign saying No Trespassing and there seems to be no other possibility to come any closer. Which has its reasons? So, I attune with my back against the outer walls of the castle. *Marquise de Beau – of Haut* – I hear and then something else. Images come up from underground passageways. This building is situated on an energetically very important place and has a huge effect on me - it must have played an important role in the century-long guarding of what is present in the mountain.

I wouldn't be surprised if here is one of the 12 secret entrances to the Temple. Everything breathes the atmosphere of secret meetings.

149

I can see the Templars entering here before my mind's eye. Probably, there was a different building in their time, but it's the same spot.

Later, when I'm back home and writing down this story, I get very sick. I have to lay down and I receive images of the Book of Love of Yeshua. The authentic book has been copied several times and I see how beautiful drawings are being added to the text. On the cover there is some kind of gemstone that radiates light; the book is surrounded by a haze of light and information. It is charged with divine energy.
Ceremonial images around the passing over of Mary Magdalene come up. And of underground passageways that leave the temple in the four wind directions and branch out in three passageways each, which makes 12 entries in all. One of those entries is coming out under the church of Rennes-le-Chateau.
Whether this is all based on truth is something I probably won't find out as long as I'm on Earth. But that's not what's it about. In such processes and kinds of alignment a lot more is often happening than we can comprehend, and the real reason often becomes clear only at a later stage.

When we walk further down, through one of the few deserted alleys of the village, we actual meet a living being. A remarkable dark man walks down the stairs from a small house with a sign saying Mairie.
I can't hold back my curiosity and ask him whether he knows anything about the castle and its owners. He looks at us with a surprised expression and tells us that the owner passed away not that long ago, that he was very rich and was there only occasionally and even then, only to accommodate large gatherings and cultural activities like concerts in his self-built theatre. With veiled words he speaks of a man of nobility. I know enough. This used to be a Templar or Cathar place, like the Chateau of Arques. Everyone residing there knew about the secrets of Pech Cardou. And who knows what secrets there still are today?

We drive off towards Chateau d'Arques, an impressive Cathar castle situated on a remarkable and distinctive place, also on a ley line. All the other Cathar castles are like insurmountable fortresses on high mountains or similar inaccessible places. This castle is connected

Chateau d'Arques, on the open field opposite Pech Cardou

with Pech Cardou and with the castle in Serres. It feels like we have to pick up an energetic key here. So, we pop up inside and connect with the energy before we continue our journey towards Arques.

Everywhere in the Languedoc we find sculptures of Joan of Arc. She's listed in the history books as a daughter of a poor farmer. Well, I don't believe that. I think she was a high initiate, maybe even coming from Arques. She also knew about the holy bloodlines and the Grail. It is more than a nice story that, in connection with the voice of God, she kept a true descendant of Charles VII on the throne.

When we drive through Arques, we stop at the only café that serves food. We see a reasonable salad buffet, the owner sitting next to it smoking and listening to weird pop music that seems completely out of place here. A little reluctantly, we take a break on the roof terrace.

I'm getting a bit impatient; it is about time for something to happen that has to do with our presence here. So, after a quick lunch, we drive back from Arques towards Serres and Pech Cardou.

Exactly opposite the portal that is called The Gate of Atlantis I park the car. We take a towel out, put it down on the tarmac, sit down on it and connect ourselves to this gate. Yes, I get confirmation that this is a stepping stone to what we are about to do, without knowing what it is. There seems to be more than one portal here, towards different dimensions. I inwardly say, *Take me to what is right for this moment.*

It becomes very quiet and a blue haze comes over my upper chakras. For some reason I am sure that this is enough to be able to continue. So, back we go, with Pech Cardou on our left. We could climb up the mountain. However, it feels like today everything wants to be effortless. Climbing isn't a part of that. A small path to the left, at the foot of the mountain takes us to a flowing source. This spot feels feminine and right, this is where 'it' may happen.

While the sun is high in the sky, we dip our feet into the clear and cold water. Yes, this is it! We talk a little about all that we have experienced today up until now. And about the S&R that we have seen in several churches. Is it about Sang Real (royal bloodline)? Or *Seigneur et Reine*? Whereupon I say: "But this is SeR! When you put this together in reverse, you get SERRES!" Later I discover that Serres is derived from the Celtic word for star.

We get lost in our own thoughts, pondering and splashing in the water at the foot of Pech Cardou. A need for silence arises naturally.

Rialsesse, place of baptism at Pech Cardou, Serres

Yeshua holding a special sphere

We sink into a meditation and are being taken, by the water, to the entrance of the mountain; a beautiful golden light portal. Mary Magdalene's energy is in front of us and Yeshua's behind us. I'm allowed to see things in the alleyways of the Temple. After a ritual cleansing in a crystal cave, we are taken to the top of the mountain. There is (also in real life) a stone circle. In the middle of this circle an energetic entrance points straight down, deep into the mountain. Here, I am guided towards a stone, enveloped by an Ark-like box.

Reverence and a feeling of greatness come over me. I consciously open my lower chakras and I clearly feel that I should make contact with the stone through my womb. A flow of love and light is going back and forth between me and the stone in the etheric Ark. This takes a while, and time ceases to exist. I realise that I'm doing something that I've done before, without my personality knowing what exactly I'm doing. *After that, words come like; Forever protected;*

You can let go of old fears about loss; and *We are eternally connected.*
A little later I open my eyes; A butterfly, a dragonfly and a little lizard are sitting with us. In the water under my feet, it looks like there is a snake curled up. It's a log, but one would swear it's a real snake. Next to me is a large stone broken in two halves, the nerve still exactly fitting. Everything shows divine presence and oneness. When I ask how we can round off this energetic work today, I hear that we can connect with the codes of the Temple-water by baptising each other in it. Wow this sounds incredibly beautiful. And it comes in handy now that I put our bikinis into our bags before we left this morning. We quickly undress. What a joyful happening this is! As always during this journey, we are completely by ourselves at this essential moment. When we had sat down here this afternoon, a man drove down towards us, turning into the little path, but he disappeared again while waving at us. We felt blessed for our sacred ritual.

Slowly, I touch the bottom of the river with my toes. The soft wet sand greets my feet. Eva looks at me expectantly and I align with her to feel what wants to come through for her. We baptize each other in this clear water, which gives us little stars of gold and shafts of light. In the beginning it feels solemn but we soon splash around and welcome each other as Princesses of the Grail on this Earth.

Later, once we are back at home, other ladies in bikinis on the field in front of our apartment invite us to join them. We are fully stretched out on the grass in the sun, full of the experience of being baptized and feeling very fulfilled. When Jaap brings us a chilled local white wine, the one we bought on our way to the caves, I know what it is like to live as Goddesses in France (a Dutch expression).

The Sacré Coeur

When you drive from Les Labadous to RLC you see a plateau on your left-hand side with a tower at the far end. This plateau is called the Sacré Coeur and has fascinated us from the first time we saw it. It is as if the Celts, who were here in pre-Christian times, are very tangible here. But the energy takes you back even further. Several mediums have sensed the presence of a Lemurian temple here, 46,000 years old. Others have seen or felt possible residences of Mary Magdalene, Yeshua or Essene friends. For centuries we have been told that Yeshua died on the cross. But the Holy Scriptures have been adapted to be suited to self-interest; the resurrection myth was ensured by the Vatican and this was the end of the story. But is this truly what happened? Many (secret) clues in the Languedoc point to the fact that Yeshua was taken off the cross

On the way to the Sacré Coeur

that same night; was taken to the grave of Joseph of Arimathea; and that he travelled to the south of France in a more enlightened, transparent physical state after his healing.

Whatever happened, we'd like to visit this plateau and somehow it feels right to do that today. It might not be a sunny day, but maybe that is for the better because there is not much shade on the large, bare field. There are some pine trees in a V-shape, planted by Elizabeth van Buren in the late eighties as a marker for alien visitors. She was the former owner of Les Labadous and she also owned this plateau beneath RLC! She was a guardian of the sacred knowledge as well, an initiate and a highly sensitive woman. Her books are no longer available. However, her energy is still present here. I feel very connected with her, especially now we enter the Sacré Coeur.

On the way to the plateau, I hear my inner voices again. Everything that wants to stay in duality is coming out here. By speaking it out straight away it can be transformed and love can be let in. First, I have to deal with my fear of aggressive dogs because I was told a few days ago that there is a stressed dog at the neighbours, who once bit Roua. Well, put me next to an aggressive dog and for sure it will bite me because I will start sending out so much fear so it can't do anything except bite me. I was once bitten by a German Shepherd dog as a child and I also still carry memories of German Shepherds in WWII. This old fear is still being touched by any dog with a strange look in their eyes. While we walk past the neighbours, I inwardly ask for help. And guess what: no dog to be seen either on the way or on the way back. Lucky me!

Further on, the grass is longer and another fearful thought appears; the one about snakes. We were warned about them as well and I thought about what Jaap had said to us.

"Let them feel that you're coming, by stomping on the ground or tapping on the rocks with a stick and because of the vibration they will get out of your way."

I frantically start tapping on the rocks and whether it's because of the rain (according to Eva, snakes don't like rain) or because of the tapping, the snakes leave us alone.

By acknowledging how tense and vulnerable I sometimes still feel and how badly I would like to release that, I'm going into deeper surrender while walking up the hill. In this mood we reach the plateau. Once we've come closer, we're surprised to find a lonely pillar. It's windy and drizzling, I lean against the pillar, bend my knees and land on the ground.

Suddenly, I become conscious of all the effort that I have made in my life to be on Earth. And that's a lot! *I will surrender completely. I'm so fed up with my personal me still wanting so much. I'm so tired of these human fears coming in between me and my divinity, time and time again,* I hear myself confess inwardly. *I would desperately like some kind of proof of the presence of whoever. Or at least something that will make my doubts about what or who I feel disappear forever!*

All this wanting and hoping and looking for. I'm fed up with it and let myself break down. Literally, flat out, on the ground. The first cry comes out of my throat. The next one comes out of my heart. And then the last bit of ego breaks, shivering and tremoring out of my solar plexus.

Whoever is watching me laying here, I am missing you so much and if you are here, please let me feel it. Oh no, now I'm wanting something again. This inner struggle goes on for a while, until the crying slows down and I quieten down a little bit.

The fountain with the lions on the Sacré Coeur, Eva is walking in the distance

Sacré Coeur – Home

I probably picked up on the crystal energy, which makes everything that is still condensed and dual tangible. Even feeling into where this pillar comes from and what it serves doesn't seem important anymore.

Then I get sucked up, my eyes semi-closed without effort and I enter a different dimension. Through a small slit of my eyes, I see large, green mists. I'm enveloped by a love, but it is different than normal.

It is like a heavenly peace. *I can lie here forever. This is my home.* This is really what it feels like, I am home there.

With a feeling as if I'm levitating, I walk to a place where there is a man-made, but very old source. It is a fountain, with a female, round water-basin in the shape of a grail, with square walls surrounding it (firm and masculine) and in each corner a guardian lion. I sit down on one of the edges, with my feet in the dry basin and I cry again.

There are many old stones in the basin and through my tears I connect with them. I take some of them in my hands as if they understand me, as if they listen to me. With a sigh I put them back and by doing that, something is released. With closed eyes I feel the high frequencies of the fountain and the green mists seem to clear up and become crystalline.

In good faith I randomly walk into the high grass, still tapping around to protect myself against 'you-never-know'-snakes. My legs want to go faster and I let them go until I reach some remnants of a wall. At an old entrance I ask for permission to enter. A voice says, *You're very welcome, sweetheart.* The same soft, pure energy as I experienced in the cave of Mary Magdalene envelops me and makes me feel joyful. I slowly go inside, entering into what feels for me like a house that has harboured many souls.

It feels so familiar! Again, I inwardly say, *Let me sit here internally. This is my home.* A little taken aback I continue. There are many rocks lying around, all seemingly inviting me to sit down on them. I close my eyes and decide to stop demanding or thinking anything, but simply to be Mieke and feel my body in full consciousness and with full attention. Naturally, I feel myself becoming one with my heart. Through an old personal layer, there is a softness occurring that fills every cell of my being. I see several souls, beings of light, in creamy white gowns.

Enveloped by a field of love and peace I realize that I'm sitting in an Essene field of energy. This feels so intense! Yes, Mary Magdalene and Yeshua could have lived here. Who else could keep this field so loving and enlightened, eternally?
My eyes open and what I see brings up my tears again. Across from me is a thorn bush, with a rose bush next to it …
In the meantime, Eva walks back from the tower; she did her own rituals there. With tears in my eyes, I show her what is in front of us. She stands behind me, lays her hand on my shaking shoulders and it feels like I'm in the loving community of 2000 years ago. This is how we lived together, stood by each other, we shared the secret knowledge and lived for the greater good. We were of service to the world from this divine love and we kept this consciousness alive within each other. We were able to bring it to the outside world from the connection to this field to which we all contributed so carefully.

The renovated tower in Visigothic style

Especially this intense dedication and care was so tangible! Then Eva continues on her own track. I stand up to go towards the tower. While I'm walking, I suddenly experience the battle that has been fought over religions, how much suffering there has been and still is, in the name of whichever God. A wave of pain comes up from my own base and flames towards my throat. I feel how much I've been fighting and searching for myself, through many incarnations. My mouth opens up and some moans come out, which soon turn into cries of grief.

I can't stop, it keeps on going. As if I'm crying out all the grief and despair of the world here on the Sacré Coeur. With tears and cracks in my voice it comes to some kind of climax. When I approach the tower with my stick in my hands, the wave fades away again. It is quiet for some time and I feel how I'm part of a group that, like me, walk around in long gowns with sticks in a sacred procession. Some other sounds are coming out of me now. I start to hum in an unknown language, softly it turns into a song of prayer and supplication. It could have been Hebrew.

My head thinks, *What on earth am I doing? What is it I'm singing?* But the need to keep going is greater, so my song of the Holy Father and the Holy Mother is sounding across the plain. It doesn't stop. If a tourist watched this from a distance, I would probably look like a lost nun. But I can't stop, it is singing through me.

When I arrive at the tower, I'm coming back to planet Earth. The carved entrance reminds me of a place where Jewish people always laid their hands and said a prayer before entering somewhere. This place is ancient, no doubt about that. It feels like the right spot to ask for a blessing for my loved ones. *May all people receive help on their path to consciousness and transformation and guidance for what they ask me to share as their intentions for this place.* I do this for everyone I can think of. The number of people grows and grows, until I realize it's better to ask for peace for the whole world. It is so powerful, so guided. Again, sounds come, while I walk away, into the high grass. "Aaaamen, aaaaahaaaaamen" and "Shaaaaaalhooooom" I sing. I don't care whether the whole village of Rennes-le-Château can hear me or not.

Unexpectedly, I arrive at a different stack of stones. The energy here is very different from the other 'house'. Everything becomes very silent within me and I feel a serene sacredness coming up. *This was one of Yeshua's spots,* I hear. There are stones to sit down on. It starts to rain again and a wind is coming up, but it doesn't bother me. Nobody can take me away from this spot now. In silence I turn inwards and express my gratitude for what Yeshua means to me personally. But also, about what he did for the whole world. He showed the loving, divine path towards consciousness. I tell him that I would like to surrender every cell of my body to this path. That I'm choosing truth and hope to shatter any illusion. That I would like to get rid of any hypocrisy that is still present in me. Complete surrender. "Into your hands I commend my Spirit."

I'm in a different state of mind, my eyes drip and the wind calms down and for some time I am at one with the emptiness that at the same time feels like 'the whole'.

Then an impulse comes for me to stand up. When I open my eyes, I see something laying in front of me, in the high grass. It is a stone, split in three parts, with a red heart on it. *The Holy Heart* passes through my mind. How does that heart get on that stone? Did some earlier spiritual visitor leave this behind? And those three parts; the Holy Trinity? It looks like an old stone. *Well,* a voice within me says, *Feel what this stone confirms for you, it doesn't matter how it got here.* This touches me. And I immediately feel that I would never dare to make the bold claim that this used to be a spot of Yeshua. It's way too holy for that... what if it isn't true... (However, one year and many books later, I know that it made sense what I felt there).

I ask for permission to take the three-part stone with me. Suddenly, I hear Eva calling out, "Mum, where are you?" She has got cold and it's time to go back. I'm vibrating in all my cells and know that we

Les Labadous, Rennes-le-Chateau

have experienced a highlight closure of our Grail journey. Fulfilled with gratitude, we walk back; back to a mug of hot soup; and a couch and bed to integrate and process all this.

When I went out later that night to write on the veranda, I bump into Tom Kenyon. It's not the first time that I meet him outside. So far, he has been walking around in a silent cocoon of imaginary invisibility, like the world isn't able to see him when he moves about between his apartment and car in a trance.

"Bonjour!" (Good day!) I enthusiastically shout a little too loudly for this late hour. He looks up with a surprised expression on his face. Straight away I ask him, "Are you on retreat, or just feeling? "Just feeling," he answers. I tell him, still full of the experiences of the day, that the energy at the Sacré Coeur is very special. He smiles and agrees.

Because I notice that he is in a deep inner alignment, I wish him a beautiful night and I think he walks on, but in fact, he stays where he is and asks me, "Have you been to the Sacred Valley already? The energy there is wonderful. Really special!" I look back and in those few seconds our energy fields seem to exchange information. "Not yet, but I will, thank you," I say. Quietly, we both go our separate ways.

Be a Book of Love

After cleaning up and packing our bags with mixed feelings, but also having the small comfort of knowing that I will come back here one day, we have one last thing to do here; to visit the Sacred Valley and find out what wants to be experienced there. I noticed this valley before. In fact, I wanted to turn off into it yesterday when we were on our way to the Sacré Coeur, just to be able to have a peak into it. But Eva reminded me that we were on our way to the plateau and that was the right thing to do in that moment.

I didn't know at that moment that Tom, the first person who I met in this heaven on Earth, would unexpectedly cross my path with these words about this valley. I didn't need any further encouragement. Eva and I are feeling quite vulnerable today. Full of all the impressions and energetic downloads that we have been received almost daily. Nevertheless, we both feel an urge to go to the valley. With our feet in our much too warm hiking shoes again and with a stick in our hands - to be able to let the snakes know that we're coming - we head off to the valley. Wow, what beautiful cliffs, the colours are mesmerizing, what a magical place!

To our left there's a lovely stream. Unfortunately, we can't reach it. But the sound of it gives refreshment in this warm valley. When we follow the path that winds beneath the Sacré Coeur, we run into a fence.

We initially see this as a sign not to continue; maybe they sometimes close the fence when work needs to be done in the valley? We weren't going to make any effort that afternoon; that's what we had agreed on. Besides, I wouldn't feel comfortable walking somewhere if there were fences like this one, or No Entry signs, unless I knew it was allowed to go there. Eva walked back to the water and looked for a spot in the shade to sit down and align herself; it's too hot to do a meditation in a sunny spot. But I'm getting drawn towards what is behind the fence…

A couple with a dog is walking up and we wonder what they will do once they reach the fence. If they go through it, we might do the same. But they turn around when they are halfway to the gorge and leave us in doubt. We walk towards the fence again. In the distance, on the cliffs to our left, we can perceive the caves of Mary Magdalene and Yeshua. We recognize the small path in white chalk that leads to the caves.

I can suddenly see it clearly now, how they descended from their living quarters at the Sacré Coeur, walking through this valley to their caves to be able to become one with the invisible worlds and to do 'their own things'. Everything breaths a sacred presence, as if they are still here …
Even though we still didn't feel completely at ease (and this is such a weird discrepancy!) we slip through the narrow gap next to the fence into the valley anyway. It's feels like we're coming into a space beyond time, and I wouldn't be surprised if some old acquaintances

View on the caves above the Sacred Valley

in linen gowns turned up around the corner.

But when we've walked into the valley for quite a while, I'm starting to doubt again. All we have seen so far are mainly thick dried out cowpats, some horse manure and very little shade. The sun is burning down on us and I'm getting restless; it feels like we are going against the flow. Eva tells me that there are often wild cows and horses in this area. Now my doubts grow even more intense.

"How can I start to align from this restlessness? I don't feel at ease anymore. Let's go back and look for a suitable place closer to the fence." So, that's what we do. We walk back and we are both inwardly looking for the message behind these sudden doubts.

When I look at the hill of the Sacré Coeur, to the left of me, I can see a beautiful spot. It's a little above us and close to the fence. If some wild animals turn up, we can quickly duck behind the fence again. I realise that it's crazy to have these kinds of thoughts in this place. But they are there, even though they are connected with old parts of me: they are there and at this moment they're not getting out of the way.

Eva nestles herself into the spot first and starts the ritual as we know it by now; camera and water bottle within reach, putting sunscreen on the parts of the body that the sun reaches. Relieved that we've found our spot, I'm about to sit down too.

But suddenly Eva shrieks. "What is happening?", I ask her. She shrieks again! When I get closer, I find her sitting next to a bush which swarms with big ants. And they have discovered her.

That's enough. Apparently, we're not meant to be sitting behind the fence. After packing our stuff, we walk back through the gate. We'll have to make peace with a less spectacular spot to align ourselves, closer to the walking path.

When we look back on it, it is a wondrously-guided quest. But in that moment, we feel like lost players who don't know what is expected from them in this unpredictable play. It feels like the director is on a coffee break and the prompter is failing on us too.

In the end, we sit ourselves down somewhere at the edge of the field at the foot of the Sacré Coeur. There is some shade and we're happy to be at ease now. Finally, we can begin our alignment. Eva and I are both trying to deal with this strange start to the day. At the same time, the silliness of it gets to me. When I turn towards the Light World inwardly, I get a hilarious image. They are very amused about all our drama! At first, I feel a little insecure and awkward, and also a little grumpy as in, *Well you get down here yourselves, then*. But when I look around, consciously choosing for a different perspective, I see a lot of smiles around me. Yes, that's how it feels. Promptly, some birds fly over and the sound that they're making is as if they're laughing at us, "Chaaah, Chaaachaaaaah"... Eva looks at me and says, "Gosh, it seems like they're laughing at us?!"

In her face I can see a flash of our drama, viewed from above. It indeed looks quite funny. We both burst out in a liberating laugh.

"Yes, I had the same feeling, that they have amused themselves greatly while watching our drama," I say, while I finally absorb the humour of it all. And with this realisation, the tension disappears as well.

After a few deeps sighs it becomes more silent and I'm being sucked inwards.

"You know what, I will just speak out loud whatever arises in me right now. It feels like that is the thing to do now," I say out loud. Immediately, it starts flowing and the words are coming out effortlessly.

"It doesn't matter where you are, dear ones. The connection is possible everywhere and we are all there. We will always be here, in this holy land, which was one of our beloved homes on this Earth. The land that gave us so much. It pleases us that you are feeling this gratitude too."

When I look around in the valley, with the Sacré Coeur above us, a love much greater than my personal love comes into my heart. While I feel the Earth beneath me, I'm looking into a different dimension, on the same field. A voice starts to powerfully speak through me. Our attention is being carefully drawn to all the elements around us, that have always been there, and always will be there.

"Feel into the beautiful energy of this field in which you're resting. It is a bedding that Mother Earth offers us ... let yourself be cradled in it. Feel how you are one with all the different shades of green surrounding you, experience their soothing effect.

Listen... hear the birds and the crickets. They have also been present here forever; every day they are singing their songs with full dedication, which testifies of divine presence."

We become even quieter. There is only the listening. And it is truly one big splendour of sounds, so beautiful, very touching. I can hear Eva breathing deeply next to me and know that she feels touched too. I hear myself speak.

"Connect to the power of the wind, let her go through you, she's your power too!"

Again, I fall silent. But from astonishment this time because it hasn't been windy at all that day. All of a sudden, out of nothing, we feel a powerful gust of wind.

"Wooooow!!" Eva calls out.

I feel goose bumps all over my body. And again, I hear the inner voice.

"Dear Mieke, please know that you never ever have to doubt what is coming through you … I am with you, you know that, you can trust that … "

Praying Jesus (Tamara Patrick)

I'm in tears. This is the energy of Yeshua. I surrender and let it happen. He speaks.

"You can already feel the Holy Family present with you, here with you. They will greet you. Simply receive because the work has been done. You have done what needed to be done for now. We are very grateful to you!"

At first I experience some 'friends and acquaintances' who are coming towards us in long gowns. Again and again, I feel emotional when I feel the connection with each of them. So loving, so soft and so familiar. A little girl rises from the circle that I'm perceiving on the field. She seems very timid, she's got something ethereal, so pure, and she radiates a golden light. She bows for us and lays down, exactly between us, a little flower that she picked from the field. *"See,"* Yeshua says, *"how she brings you her Book of Love".* That touches us deeply because this is how our journey started, in the church of Rennes-le-Chateau, with *The Book of Love* containing the words of Yeshua himself.

"This is how simple the highest truth can look like in its Earthly shape. This is how simple she is. God lives in each small part; we live in God. This transcends every Earthly limitation! Each one of us finds his or her own way of expressing this. But you always recognise it because it carries the divine truth. Be a Book of Love! Live a Book of Love! Write a Book of Love! The world needs it; this light wants to be transmitted. Know that your intention - to connect with the all-compassing universal field of consciousness and love - is enough."

I can hear Eva sighing. She is listening carefully and in a very perceptive state with all her senses attuned. Making myself as receptive as possible, I feel almost tangibly touched by a very tender energy. My skin feels pearlescent, so radiant and I can perceive the same soft radiance that I felt in the cave of Mary Magdalene.

"Yes, I'm Mary Magdalene, as you knew me. I'm here in your company too, in gratitude, on this holy spot. Dear sisters, thank you for your deep trust in the divine guidance - I've experienced that here too. We're sharing the poignancy of this moment, the love of the sacred mother's bosom, the purity of the Goddess. Know that I will always be with you."

I feel how a certain sweet presence anchors in my lower belly. It's hard to put it into words, it's so precious, so serene. So completely

170

Mary Magdalene

different from the image that we carried within ourselves, as ungodly women, about our femininity.

In the meantime, an older man rises up from the circle of those present, diagonally to the right from me. He radiates an endearing love, wisdom and warmth. Everything within me reacts to his energy. Tears are flowing over my cheeks and I know: this is Joseph of Arimathea. The inner voice comes through me again.

"Receive, dear daughters, his blessing. This power, that is given to you now, will stay with you forever. It is a connection from the highest divinity that will be connected to Earth through your bodies."

We bow our heads to be able to feel even deeper within ourselves, to be able to surrender our personalities ever more fully to this great moment.

I also notice a car that is driving towards us. That is unusual because there are only walking trails here. I'm half-looking in its direction and see a white car with red bands (Police?) It looks like a Templar shield! The car stops under a tree and then nothing happens.

"Know that there are angels surrounding this field, like guardians and protectors around the circle of loved ones. It will always be this way. Live this great consciousness that is within you. Be the light in the world. Love your physical body, so that wisdom, power and the crystal Grail energy can penetrate even more deeply into it. Let your fellow human beings taste of the living waters of the divine source. Let it bubble and fizz through you!

Rise now and remember, Goddesses. Rise before the eye of all your loved ones. We rise together with you, in this moment, in this sacred valley at the Sacré Coeur. Feel in your hearts how you are connected with us.

We understand your human doubts and pains. But rise, be this circle, be this truth! Step very consciously out of the old snake skin, shaped by nothing else than the divinity of us all!

Rise in the new Light of a new world!

And when you feel ready, dedicated to this magnificent Light, as a living witness of the Book of Love, to help build a new world: then let the Yes come from your heart. Let this truth become audible in the world. Let this sound be heard over the holy land!"

Clearly, feeling deeply touched by this, we both say, "Yes". Carefully at first, but it becomes more and more powerful. We are lifted by the

New Light in the Sacred Valley

energy of that huge circle present in this field and we are not the only ones shouting Yes!

The more conscious we become of this, the more joyful our crying out becomes. As above, so below; we are all standing hand in hand, and we simultaneously start singing, "Shaaaaalooooom".
While the tears are flowing down our cheeks, our eyes slowly open. We find each other and fall into each other's arms. It feels like it's not just us, but the whole world around us is looking anew. What a Light, what a tenderness! It isn't my daughter I see now. I see the Goddess in her. Still on a high, we thank the Light World and take photographs of the spot and each other. Then we walk back, feeling into what happened, while part of us still remains in that other world.

The first thing to get us back in the here and now is the car that drove up while we were halfway in our alignment; it is still there. We didn't see anyone come out of the car and in fact, the driver is still in there and has been a witness of all that happened. We meet friendly eyes that are trying to figure us out. It is very fitting

The Accolade, Edmund Blair Leighton

what he came to do when we read what is shown on his car: *Eau potable communale*. He came to do maintenance on the source of the communal drinking water there, whose entrance is just before the fence.

While we smile at him in a friendly manner, we become conscious of the fact that he has witnessed our whole process; next to my talking into the space, he also must have heard our screaming out, "Yes!" Our jumping around in the field and the "Shaaaloom" singing. Wonderful and all that time he stayed at the edge of the field, like a Templar, allowing us to stay aligned.

It becomes even funnier when, while we are chatting together about goddesses, a group of young men with beautifully bronzed torsos walk towards us. They look like junior Chippendales! While we greet and pass each other laughing, they appear to be young Dutch gods who have an immediate crush on the young goddess next to me.

Once we are back at Les Labadous, we're so impressed by everything that has happened that we don't do anything at all for the rest of the day. This closure of the week in this sacred land is something we need to allow to sink in very deeply and read about again and again.

La Cité, Carcassonne

PART THREE:

The Netherlands

Epilogue

I could continue writing. About how hard it was to leave Rennes-le-Chateau and come back to the three-dimensional world and about all the tourist madness in Carcassonne. About how rich we felt to be able to land back on Dutch soil with all these new experiences and which, also because of all the notes and pictures we took, we could revisit it all from our home. About how we have both been integrating this day and night, to round off the processes that started up there and for me - to get them down on paper – and into this book to share with you.

What is truly interesting for us all, you and me, is the message that Yeshua, Mary Magdalene and all the other Holy Quest seekers gave us that day.

"Rise and remember yourself."

With all my heart I hope that this book can contribute to this mission. That within you something is touched while you read this book; an ancient knowing opens up and you start to remember. That something within you will be able to hear the call from the Light, to find the love, the knowledge and the power that have all been given to us to find our way back home and to use this in our daily lives.

Thank you, my dear Eva; that you are in my life; that you remind me of who I truly am; and that you made this journey with me from your purest Being.

Thank you, my dear friend, Vincent; for your unconditional presence; your wisdom; and the loving holding space that you offered me, which makes it possible for me to meet and learn to truly love all aspects of myself.

Thank you, my dear parents, sister and friends; for your trust in me; for the constant support and encouragements to follow my own path.

Thank you, all of you; for your daily sharing, mirroring and feedback; for your touching enthusiasm for this book from the first to the last word.

Special thanks to; Joke, Franklin, Jaap and Axel for their heart-warming home at Les Labadous, which has now been transferred into the loving hands of Christine and Martin, Aafke and Johan, who will guard this sacred place from now on; Luke for his warm permission to use his *Comme Une* (As One) painting; Tamara for her warm permission to use her Praying Jesus painting; Gordon, for his immediate welcoming of my book and articles on his enlightening website www.nieuwetijdskind.com

Bye Bye, Joke & Franklin

179

Hen Straver

On the day that my first printed book in Dutch was published, Hen Straver died. He was my first therapist and teacher. Together with Lenne Gieles he set up the Academy for Transformation work, where I was both a pupil and a teacher, during a period of 14 years. Our soul connection is an old and deep one.

He sometimes called me his adopted daughter. His all-compassing Christ consciousness and reincarnation work has touched me deeply. Dear Hen, thanks so much for being in my life, as a spiritual father, who always supported me when it was about this sacred work. We will stay in touch and you can count on me for continuing this work with heart and soul.

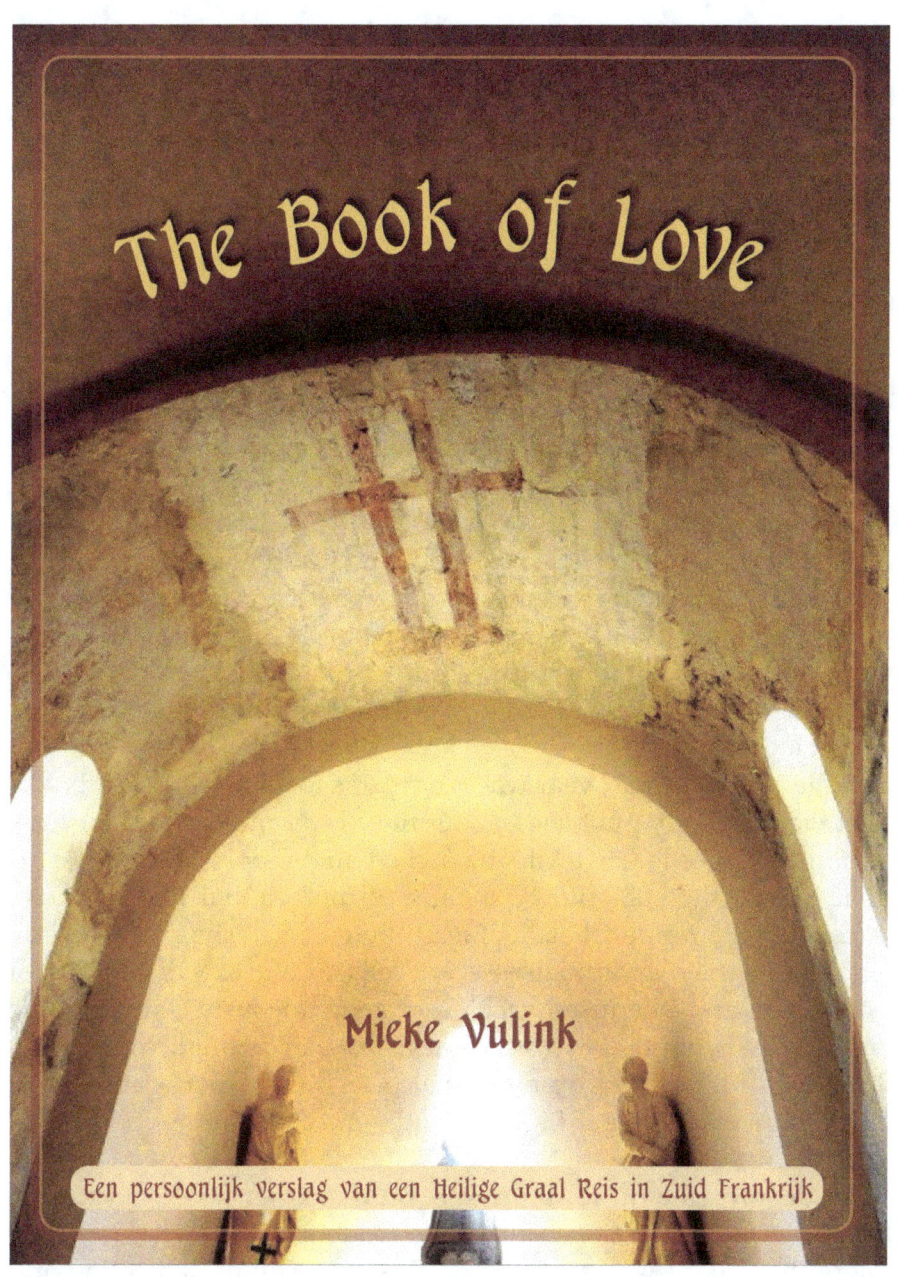

The Book of Love

Mieke Vulink

My first, self-made Book of Love, 2015

Epilogue 2016

It has been a year since this book was first published in the Dutch language. My life has really taken off since then. Whereas I previously had no clue what the meaning of this book was and whether or not it should be printed, I'm now working on a second edition.

About a 100 articles have come through me in the past year, in a continuous flow of inspiration and soulfulness. Hours of work, all pro-bono, but all coming from truth and the drive of the moment itself.

Where my practice for self-realisation and healing has rapidly taken shape, I now feel that newer, different forms are on their way. Some experiences described in the book I would experience differently now, and also put them in different words. But I have decided to leave the text as it is, so it remains as pure as it was during this Holy Quest journey.

A huge gift in the past year was what came to me when I read books that were recently published about the Holy Family and their lives around Rennes-le-Château. It touched me deeply when I heard that indeed there should be a copy of the original Book of Love present in Rennes-le-Château. I read about how Yeshua was secretly baptised at the river at Rialsesse, at Pech Cardou; exactly at the spot where Eva and I baptised each other spontaneously. And how the villa across from there was indeed a Templar stronghold. And so, I received further confirmation that placed my experiences in this book in an even greater Light of truth – no capital there, so greater light of truth.

I am deeply grateful for all that is on the paper here, and for the heart-warming reactions of all my readers. I can't say anything more than that I will continue on this path full of dedication and surrender.

♥

Inspiration

Epilogue 2019

Nothing within me was aware of the fact that four years later I would make another journey to Rennes-le-Château again, this time with Vincent. I knew I had lived with him in this area more than 2000 years ago; we used to be a Grail couple. It was exciting to find out whether he would feel the same connection with this sacred land. This soon became clear; he, too, felt himself coming home here.

We had brought a few Dutch copies of this book. They were joyfully welcomed at Hotel les Costes in Montségur (unfortunately this hotel closed his doors in 2020), in the B&B Canigou Lodge at Mount Canigou, in Les Labadous and in the book shops of Rennes-le-Château.

When we got back from our journey, people offered to translate the book into English and French. I neither thought nor expected that this would ever happen.

Two months later, in the late summer of 2019, I received a message from a woman who was following my articles. With my Dutch book under her arm, she was with her friend and her friend's husband in Rennes-le-Château. The husband was the owner of the Dutch publishing company Oorsprong (meaning Origin). He asked if he could get in touch with me when he returned. As I'm writing this, the publishing contract is ready and the Dutch version of *A Journey to Love* is undergoing a professional rebirth to a much larger audience.

From higher hands of Love, my second book is also being created. In the meantime, Vincent and I unexpectedly went back to France on two occasions. So much was being touched and opened there that it took me some time when I got home to process all the physical 'resets'.

While writing the second book, I received the message that my books would become a trilogy. I called my publisher and he was enthusiastic about that too.

Thank you, Werner; that you had the courage to live your destiny as a publisher of spiritual books fully again. A long time ago, many holy scriptures in Ephesus have been preserved thanks to you. It is an honour that my Dutch books are in your hands!

The higher, unconditional love-field that has been activated again will spread among more and more people. Old acquaintances and lovers will rejoice, with one goal: to bring the Christ consciousness back into ourselves and onto Earth.

Bless You.
Zutphen, 22-11-2019

May the road rise to meet you
May the wind be always at your back
May the sun shine warm upon your face
And may the rain fall soft upon your fields
And, until we meet again
May God hold you in the hollow of his hand

**